Buffalo in the 1970's is very much a big-league town. Teams from three of the most respected major sports leagues in the nation play here—and they play to win. But all this success didn't happen overnight in Buffalo. Ralph Hubbell—known to friends and fans as "Hub"—has C been calling it like it is for well on to 40 years in Buffalo, and he's the man who remembers it all.

In *Come Walk With Me,* Ralph, long western New York's best-known sportscaster, chronicles, in warm-hearted anecdotes and fond memories, the development of big-time sports in Buffalo. He also re-counts his own development in a delightfully personal autobiographical section, and then presents, for the first time, his own "one man's Hall of Fame" . . . which includes first-person recollections and inter-

(continued on back flap)

(continued from front flap)

views with some of the greatest athletes, and greatest characters, of all time.

Come Walk With Me also traces the development of Buffalo's Big Three through "Hub's" eyes: The Buffalo Bills, who, with Lou Saban, Jack Kemp, and now O.J. Simpson, not only establishing unrivalled superiority in the old AFL, but are now, surely, headed for the top in the NFL . . . the Sabres, with Gil Perreault, Rick Martin, and the late Tim Horton, who have made the former "expansion club" a power to be reckoned with in the NHL . . . the Braves of Bob McAdoo, Ernie DiGregorio, and Eddie Donovan, a team which is establishing itself as the best young club in the NBA.

But Ralph Hubbell's *Come Walk With Me* is perhaps most stirring in its warm and sentimental recollections of a life filled with love, kindness, and an abiding belief in the goodness and dignity of all people. The "Hub" is a uniquely talented and wonderful man—and this *Walk* reflects those qualities.

Come Walk With Me

RALPH HUBBELL

PRENTICE-HALL, INC., Englewood Cliffs, New Jersey

Come Walk With Me
by Ralph Hubbell
Copyright © 1975 by Ralph Hubbell
Printed in the United States of America
Prentice-Hall International, Inc., London
Prentice-Hall of Australia, Pty. Ltd., Sydney
Prentice-Hall of Canada, Ltd., Toronto
Prentice-Hall of India Private Ltd., New Delhi
Prentice-Hall of Japan, Inc., Tokyo

10 9 8 7 6 5 4 3 2 1

Library of Congress Cataloging in Publication Data

Hubbell, Ralph,
    Come walk with me.

    1. Hubbell, Ralph,   2. Radio broadcasting
of sports.   3. Television broadcasting of sports.
4. Sports—Biography.   I. Title.
GV719.H82A33   070.4'49'7960924   74-30325
ISBN 0-13-152520-4

Introduction

For most mortals, bonds with fellow human beings are as strong as memories. But for many, these bonds diminish as new friends and people capture their attention and memories dim.

Ralph Hubbell is an extraordinary man with an uncanny memory enriched with the perspective of time and events.

Why he is so endowed is a source of wonderment. But it is my belief that Ralph's interest and enjoyment in people, indeed his love for mankind, are overriding reasons for his rare talent.

Since he began his broadcasting career in Buffalo forty years ago, Ralph has been a household word in western New York and adjacent areas of Ontario. In many teams' locker rooms and in the front offices of America's great, well-known, lesser, and local sports clubs, and among his peers in the sportscasting business, he's deserved and received tremendous respect for his ability, his dedicated fairness, and most of all his amazing capacity to understand his fellow human beings.

He has been a friend of Joe McCarthy and other legendary figures of sports history and has not only chronicled their careers and those of lesser known athletes, but has formed kindred relationships beyond the usual acquaintanceships that other writers seek and enjoy.

Ralph Hubbell followed Sugar Ray Robinson from the time he was a spindly-legged amateur through his capture of the lightweight, welterweight, and middleweight titles. While other scribes and sportscasters perceived Sugar Ray's closeness with his trainer, George Gainsford, it was Ralph who discovered why the gifted boxer never rode the elevator from the twelfth floor of Buffalo's Statler-Hilton Hotel.

The reason, which Ralph found and disclosed to fight fans, was that Robbie was afflicted with claustrophobia—not really a handicap for a boxer whose opponents sought to corner in the ring.

The deeply sensitive Ralph agonized while his friend Ben Hogan struggled back from the auto accident that crushed his legs and pelvis. Ralph rejoiced at Hogan's comeback spree, which included wins in the Masters, PGA, and U.S. and British Opens tournaments. And Ralph was there when such youngsters as Jack Nicklaus and Arnold Palmer moved in to take over Hogan's world.

Ralph shared with his audiences his fascination with the awesome power and other gridiron feats of such running backs as Marion Motley, Jim Brown, and my former teammate and friend, Cookie Gilchrist.

"There would not be a hospital big enough to house the lame and the halt" if a coach were able to put the three in a single backfield, Ralph once speculated.

Basketball, hockey, horse racing, six-day bicycle racing—any sport at any level which smacked of genuine competitiveness, achievement, adversity, and opportunities grasped and bypassed—have been Ralph's forte.

Ralph Hubbell "retires" from one medium to begin a new career in another. He has traveled from radio to television, back to radio, and on to writing books and columns.

To the reader unfamiliar with his character, mind, and works, his prose is a rich treasure discovered.

Who but Ralph Hubbell would feel inspired to essay his personal interpretation of "America, the Beautiful"?

To the Duluth-born Ralph, the lines "O beautiful for spacious skies" mean "Clear, blue skies to beckon our eyes and beseech us to look up with pride in this land of ours and beyond, with reverence and hope, to God Almighty who forgives us our troubled times in the knowledge that our ship is a proud ship and that our way is a proud and progressive way—and is not a lost way."

Or would any other American, speaking for our country, equate *"and crown thy good with brotherhood"* with such thoughtful words as *"It is the acceptance of each other as a brother but not just within the circle of our own family. Brotherhood goes beyond our shores and insists that we accept all people as brothers, for all people, one day, must be free."*

Ralph Hubbell is a man among men with a beautiful gift, a one-of-a-kind person who bids from his heart Come Walk With Me. *I'm honored to be his friend.*

JACK KEMP, *Member of Congress*

Foreword

The profile of a nation is the collective profile of its people. Therefore, it is not a contention but a conviction that it is not the incident along the way that counts, but the person or persons responsible for it. We remember the man more than the moment, and because of this I offer you this book in the fervent hope, and candid belief, that you will enjoy meeting those people who have been the architects of my life in the fertile areas of western New York and a segment of the Province of Ontario, Canada.

The pages of this book, as bare as an un-Pampered infant such a short while ago, now contain the life story of a man whose radio career started in 1931, who embraced the world of sportscasting in 1935, responded to the ham within him when television blinked a little red light in 1948, and continued on the home screen until September 1970.

My walk through the years has been such a delightful experience, people from all areas of life have been so fascinating, that I simply decided that I'd ask you to journey with me. Maybe, in helping me recapture much of my life, you will find a great deal of yours as well. So forget what it is that you figure needs forgetting, and come walk with me.

Contents

TO A.B.H.

MOST IMPORTANT OF ALL

and

to the memory of

Philip Welch Hubbell

1

As It Was in the Beginning

RADIO BECKONED EARLY IN MY LIFE BUT the time for my entry wasn't quite at hand. Either I was too young to realize my potential in the medium, or radio, as an industry, seemed too insecure as a livelihood for me. My second year after high-school graduation—while the world was stymied by possibly its worst, and certainly its most far-reaching depression—I came to Buffalo from Brooklyn, where my secondary-school years were, academically, rather misspent. They were pleasant years, meager years, with not much accomplished book-wise but with a tremendous emphasis placed on sports. This indulgence in sports, combined with a sort of inborn fascination for declamation and poetry, brought out what I later considered to be my most potent asset, the Hubbell ham. Ultimately it all was parlayed into a sportscasting career, the start of which, as you will see, was delayed by constant detours caused by two things: first, the lack of a definite career objective, and second, the immediate necessity for eating.

In 1929, 1930, and 1931, had you been there, you would have realized that if bank presidents were selling polished apples, freshwater high-school graduates were turning a buck through the use of mirrors and other kindred forms of magic. Those first two

1

years saw me as a typewriter salesman (I sold one portable), as a switchboard operator at the Downtown Y in Brooklyn (in exchange for my room), as the manager of a hotel on Sixth Avenue in Manhattan, (the story of that seven-week career would fill a second book), as a salesman for Quaker Oats in the Bronx, and as a bystander (my chief diversion, but without pay) watching the Empire State Building rise on Fifth Avenue.

Late in 1930, my beloved Aunt Emily put me on the road to purposeful thinking. For when my mother died in 1919 Tem, which was all we ever called her, simply changed the entire pattern of her life with a selfless dedication and raised her sister's three boys, Albert, Philip, and Ralph. At the time of Mother's death we lived in Buffalo, and Tem lived with us. She was always a devout woman, and her affiliation with Westminster Presbyterian Church in Buffalo not only gave greater meaning to that church, but it was to play a tremendous part in my life. Just as 1931 broke, Tem suggested that it might be wise if I contacted Westminster with an eye toward a career in working with youngsters less fortunate than I. The church operated what is still a fine institution, the Westminster Community House, and so I applied for part-time employment there. Without any actual experience, but blessed with ebullient enthusiasm and a basic knowledge of athletics—along with a real affection for youngsters—I approached one rotund individual with the stage name, or so it sounded, of Fairfax Gordon Steele. Fax, as we referred to him, was Director of Boys' Work there and a man who was dearly loved by all who came under his spell. When his boys' activity career ended, he went to Elmira, New York, to sell antiques, and the last I heard Fax was still in business although he must—as, eventually, with all of us—come under the heading of antique himself today.

Though such a beginning may seem humble in light of this years-later reflection, it served as a leveling process. I leveled with myself most of all, for I learned at that early stage the importance of compassion—especially for young men and women. The learning was far from easy because there was so much with which to contend yet I am happy for that. I have always felt that the very nature of the obstacles forced us to learn faster and more.

When I presented myself to Fax Steele and declared myself a fledgling with no experience, he said, "The pay will be twenty-seven dollars a month." That seemed fair, especially in view of the fact that my only income to that point in life was a weekly dole from Tem and even she admitted that the word should have been spelled "weakly." What Mr. Steele said to me after I told him that I would take the job caused me to pause: "Your board and room will be thirty dollars a month." All of the computer geniuses in the world can't subtract thirty dollars from twenty-seven dollars and still come up with a plus. But I had to have this job, and I was doggoned if I was going to let this guy know my straits and just as doggoned if I would ask Tem for one cent to make up the differ-ence. So I took the job, and now—and I can almost smell this— you are waiting to find out just how that difference was made up.

The first thing I did was to go in search of something to do, however menial, that would not conflict with my work at West-minster. My job there required being on duty during the evenings and some afternoons, but I had my mornings free plus Saturdays and Sundays. Street pounding was rarely productive in those days, and so when I caught on with Kleinhans Men's Store I considered myself extremely fortunate. Mind you, I did not begin as an executive—nor did I finish as one. As a matter of simple fact, I had a dual position: hauling up stock from the basement and cleaning the showcases. My hours were nine to nine each Saturday, and the stipend was a fat two dollars every Saturday. This still left me a buck shy of my required thirty dollars, but I was on my way even though I almost blew the job the first day I was given it.

Fulfilling my obligation to Kleinhans was a simple thing at best. It required me to bring the goods from the basement to whatever floor was designated via an oversized basket equipped with wheels. In order to negotiate the route, it was necessary to wheel along a seemingly endless corridor to the freight elevator. My job couldn't be classified as one of vital importance, to be sure, but *someone* had to cart that stuff up so it could be sold, and, right then, I was that someone. My attitude has always had much of the adventurer about it, so after I had safely negotiated three or four trips, I looked about for some diversion. After all, pushing a basketful of clothes can get pretty dull at two bucks per twelve-hour day. In the exuberant spirit of a man who has finally started the long road up, I gave vent to my enthusiasm. Very simply, I piled my cart with clothes and then steered my steed to the corridor. Next, we went into high gear, and as we jet propelled toward the elevator I climbed aboard. Suddenly I spied the form of a man entering my course from a side doorway. Obviously, there was no way to brake my no-brakes steed—and the ensuing collision was a beaut. The unravelling process fortunately revealed no injuries, but it did reveal my cart as being in an upside-down position and my goods piled high upon the irate, fuming, gesticulating person whom I had almost cut in half.

You will come to know that I have never done anything in my life by half-measure—and I didn't that day, either. Perish the thought that I would fell an auditor, a salesman, an electrician, or a brother stockroom boy. The individual who was almost belted into oblivion was John Steurnagel, president of Kleinhans Men's Store, who turned out to be one of the nicest guys in the world. Of course I didn't know that just then, but when he didn't fire me I decided it was so. Yet, though he didn't fire me, he didn't let the incident go without notice either. As a matter of fact, he gave me the finest tongue-lashing ever administered outside a woodshed, and even today I can repeat it almost word for word.

So far we have accounted for twenty-nine of the thirty dollars I needed to pay room and board. Further pavement pounding proved fruitless, which meant I needed either one of two things: a stroke of good fortune or adroit planning based on cunning with, ultimately, a sticky finger in the till. Fortunately, my smile from Lady Luck came as I was nearing the first rent payment.

It was a morning in January 1931, and though I can't recall the weather conditions the sun just had to be shining. I was in my

4

two-by-four suite listening to the radio. I was tuned to station WEBR in Buffalo, and some records were being spun to supplement the commercial messages of Frank Meyers' Appliance Shop. As a number played on, probably "Last Night on the Back Porch I Loved Her Best of All," the needle stuck in the record. It stuck somewhere between the singer's love for her and the back porch, but it stuck and my entire life changed as if someone, or Someone, had ordained it. As the needle stuck, my thought processes struck on an idea. A wild idea? You had better believe it. But who called the Wright Brothers sane? And who, when it was suggested that a person would pole vault eighteen feet, responded, "Sure, it'll happen in '72"?

The phone was downstairs, and I made it in one leap. My call was to Frank Meyers' Appliance Shop, and Frank answered the call. (Later I found out that if he hadn't answered it, it would still be ringing since he had no employees). A break came my way when I realized that Mr. Meyers was fuming at WEBR and this I found out in short order. You could smell the fumes. After giving my name, I said, "Mr. Meyers, I am listening to your program on WEBR and . . ."—that's as far as I got. "Don't you tell me what's happening," he bellowed, "this is about the tenth time it's happened, and I'm fed right up to here." I guessed how far up he was fed, and while I was guessing I had a sinking feeling that he might hang up. Suddenly his voice softened, and he thanked me for calling. That gave me my foot-in-the-door chance, so I said, "Would you be willing to talk to me about your program if I came down to your store?" He had cooled down considerably and suggested that he would enjoy such a visit.

About a half hour later I presented myself to Mr. Meyers and explained that I had an idea I believed would better entertain his audience, and would increase that audience, and thus would increase his sales. My idea, hastily contrived, was simply to read poetry with organ records forming a soothing background. That was a big trend during early radio years with Jesse Crawford at the organ and men with the then-magical names—Tony Wons, David

5

Ross, and Franklyn McCormack—reading poetry. It's a shame that the trend faded, for interpretive poetry can be a delightful balm for tensions and as musical to the ear as the best song ever composed. So I suggested to Frank Meyers that it be tried on a local scale, and he liked the idea immediately. He made the necessary arrangements with WEBR, and the following week the "Wandering Poet," in the guise of R. Hubbell, ambled on the radio scene of Buffalo and those parts of western New York that, at the time, could pick up that peanut whistle.

This sudden infiltration of the local radio industry by a brash upstart enabled me to accomplish two ends, although you must agree that one wasn't an end, it was a beginning. Joining hands with Frank Meyers allowed me to zoom over the rent barrier by twenty-four dollars per month since I needed only one dollar to hit the thirty-dollar total. Frank paid me twenty-five dollars a month for twenty-four half-hour programs, and if I wasn't exactly on Easy Street I was at least financially solvent and had trolley fare downtown. But the most important thing was that I had a radio program of my own. Though it can't be hailed as the start of a radio career—because in three months time I was out of Buffalo and back in Brooklyn, where I accepted the opportunity to become Director of Boys' Work for the Little Italy Neighborhood Association—1931 was my introduction to radio. And my first taste of it was a lasting one, believe me.

2

The Big Lessons at Little Italy

HIS NAME WAS LILY MANGANO. UNDOUBT-
edly Lily was a nickname, but it isn't important for he was all
young man. Mangano was spawned in the asphalt corridor that
calls itself Columbia Street, deep in the Red Hook section of
Brooklyn. It was during my first hour of employment at The Little
Italy Neighborhood Ass'n. that I met him, and so vivid is my
recollection of that day that I can hear his voice even now. When
Lily Mangano appeared in my cubbyhole office and said, "What
are you here for?," there was no greeting, no smile; just, "What
are you here for?" Before I answered, I asked myself, "That's
right, mister, what are you here for? If you know, then tell the
man."

There was no reason why I had to explain to this lad, but I
showed him more courtesy than he had shown me by giving him
my name and extending my hand. He softened, but only a wee bit,
and took my hand. Then he gave me his name and I asked him to
have a seat. He refused, as if he were holding his ground for some
strange reason. "I'm here in an effort to head up the activities of
the young boys in this section," I told him. Mangano said,
"What's wrong with the young boys of this section?" The tension
started to thicken once again, and then, incredibly, I realized that

7

this young man—I believe we were about the same age—wasn't in my office as an enemy. He had come as a friend, but with wariness that suggested he might not be accepted as one. He was, actually, one of the boys of that section who had never been helped. He had grown to maturity because he was inherently decent and he had a desire to rise above his environment. He had never known anything except the seedy side of growing up and knew only that to survive in that crime-infested area was a triumph in itself. Realizing this, I also discovered that I had found a formidable ally, because here was a young man who was no stranger to the hundreds of youngsters who would be touched by the work which I was sent to Little Italy to do.

So I simply used the oldest tactic in war or sports strategy. The best defense is a quick and sure attack. I said to my new friend, "You're here today because you believe that I, as the first to come here to help from the outside, can ignite some kind of desire for progress in a section that can't even define the word. Shake my hand hard, Lily, and together let's take it from here." As the first sight of land after a long voyage never leaves a sailor's mind the pressure of that handshake, the suddenly warm smile, and the devotion that Lily Mangano gave me over the next two years has never left me. No, after I left Red Hook, I never saw him again in person. But I have seen him a thousand times in my mind's eye.

The first meeting with Lily concluded on two vital points. He said; "You can count on me for whatever volunteer service I can give. That goes for my gang, too." Then he paused, looking far wiser than his years would indicate, and said, "Remember, Mr. Hubbell, you are here to help our boys and that should be your one thought. You will see much that you have never seen before, and you will see much that will be unlawful and you will want to do something about it. But this is a world you have never seen, and you are not here as a cop. Even the cops wish they weren't here as cops. What you do is your business, but what you will see is not. Dead heroes in Red Hook are a dime a dozen."

Lily Mangano looked me dead center in the eyes and walked

out of my office. But I felt a victory, a big victory, had been won—for when he walked out, he was smiling.

Two weeks later, I had reason to thank my young friend for his plain talk and his knowledge of his area and of what it means to mind one's own business and keep his mouth shut. My office was on the second floor of the building which consisted of one other office, for the Director, two meeting rooms, and a runt-sized gymnasium. My cubicle fronted on Columbia Street—a beehive of humanity, crowded little stores, and seemingly a thousand pushcarts from which you could purchase anything from can openers to Cadillacs—with the can openers outselling the Caddies, 50,000 to nothing. In the evening, from about eight o'clock on, the street was deserted. At about nine, it became furtive, and at eleven I closed the house. The senior boys were out by ten, and the final hour I spent in the office going over the records and the day's activities and the planning for the morrow. But it meant an hour alone and with two large French windows facing the Street I had a clear view of the dim dinginess of the night. Also, and even at my then 133 pounds, that was a pretty fair target in the office sitting at the desk.

This particular night, just two weeks after Lily's visit and just at closing time, two sharp lights heralded the arrival of a sleek limousine which came to rest directly across the way. Two men emerged and immediately went to the trunk, opened it, and hauled out what appeared to be a third individual. The gruesome threesome headed into the store which, believe it or not, was a candy hut but which in reality was just another front for whatever those guys needed a front. As the burden was borne inside, I doused my light and waited until the limousine was reoccupied and driven away. Then I walked home to Columbia Heights. It was a million miles from Columbia Street to Columbia Heights in Brooklyn. Especially that night.

At about four the next afternoon, I was told that there was a man who wanted to talk with me and who was waiting for me in my office. So I handed the referee's whistle to Mangano, now my

9

chief assistant, and he continued the activity in the gym. When I arrived, I was surprised to see a man known only as "T" waiting for me. He was the proprietor of the across-the-street candy store, and I had met him a couple of times while buying, of all things, candy. He smiled, we shook hands, and he said, "How's it going?" When I told him I thought that things had started well, he said, still smiling, "You were working late last night, and I wondered how you liked my new car?" The distant warning from the prophetic Lily Mangano set a clarion bell ringing in my ears. I said, "What car, T?" He gave me a long, long look and said, still with a smile, "We'll get along fine, Hubbell."

Once it had been established, that there was a young guy around who was taking time to help the youngsters, the swing was the other way. Many neighborhood natives became almost overly protective. Legs Diamond once told me, "I want you to take this check for $5,000 to help prevent what happened to me and a thousand others when we were too young, as these kids are too young to know better, and found feeble excuses for the wasting of the precious years." I found compassion where I never expected to find it. When you dig for silver, sometimes you find gold.

In every respect, the Little Italy Neighborhood Association cared for some three hundred youngsters every day, Mondays through Saturdays. Our major problem was health, and the conditions I found when I arrived upon the scene were too wretched to describe or to believe. At the beginning, each child—and there were no exceptions—came with a headful of nits—leechlike little fellows who dig into the scalp with a tenacity that is astounding. Each head was shaved and then washed in disinfectant—the kids would say, "I got me a watermelon haircut." The sores that the nits created were cruel to behold, but once the youngsters realized that they were going to be clean for the first time in their lives they were agreeable to anything and became dedicated to keeping clean.

Our second biggest health problem was V.D. It was my thought, when our doctor found it so prevalent in boys and girls from nine on up to eighteen, to conduct a series of lectures concerning the ramifications of this disease. As a matter of fact, we started such a program, but it was just whistling in the wind —the kids couldn't possibly know what it was all about. I hit upon the idea of group visits to the V.D. Clinic of Long Island College Hospital. There we saw the medical magic performed as the youngsters—all of them, not just the afflicted ones—were given first-hand knowledge of what it was all about. No, we never licked the disease, because the world hasn't beaten that one as yet. But we managed to end much of the promiscuity, and we had visible proof that the afflicted youngsters were benefited by medical means.

The people with whom I lived, worked, and played back in those still vivid two years in Brooklyn had one thing in common, if nothing else: They had an inherent devotion to each other. They were poor and most of them didn't have much education, but there's a lot we can still learn from them.

3

How Buffalo Entered My Bloodstream

DURING THE CHRISTMAS HOLIDAYS OF 1933, I journeyed from Brooklyn to Buffalo for the express purpose of spending this festive time with my brother Phil, who was employed by the Merchants Mutual Casualty Company. It proved to be possibly the most fortuitous trip of my life since, besides spending time with Phil, I managed to do two things that completely altered my entire approach to the future. At this juncture I believed that my dedication to social work would enable me to embrace that type of livelihood as a career. But I was too inexperienced to understand that Dame Fortune is a fickle gal and she can change your thinking—and therefore your life—with a smile or a frown. Dame Fortune has been my friend. Lady Luck has been my lover.

The first thing that happened to me occurred when I walked into a living room on Chapin Parkway, where brother Phil had lodgings, and was introduced to a young lady who was tremendously embarrassed because an infected tooth had so swollen the left side of her jaw that she appeared to have lost the battle in round one. Her name was Ann Bolton, she hailed from Cedar Rapids, Iowa, and she was visiting her aunt, who was Phil's landlady. Ann and I took an intense dislike to each other and were married a year from the following May in Cedar Rapids.

The following day, for want of something better to do, I wandered over to 735 Main Street—then the second floor home of WEBR—to say hello to those lads I had met when I was wandering around with a poetry book in my hand, organ music in my ears, and world applause in my dreams.

One of my earliest friends and the man actually responsible for my decision to make radio my career was Jack McLean. When I departed after my brief poetry stint, Jack said that if the day ever came when I might like to explore the brand-new industry of radio broadcasting, he would do everything possible to aid me. Thus, after that Christmas junket in 1933, Jack McLean not only was the first person to greet me on my return for what I thought would be a brief reunion, but he was also the fellow who, after saying hello, stated, "Death claimed one of our announcers just last week and we need a man to take his place." And so on May 28, 1934, I became a member of the announcing staff of WEBR, and I must confess that neither the world in general nor the world of radio stood still. But my heart did, for this was a great challenge in a city which already had infiltrated my bloodstream. Therefore, when Ann Bolton left Cedar Rapids, Iowa, as Ann Hubbell with me on the night of May 24, 1935, we had made one irrevocable promise to each other: We would dig deeply into the soil of Buffalo, and if we were blessed with children in the normal course of events we would grow with them in that city because we knew that we were building in an environment which had a rich heritage and which offered us vast opportunities to live a decent, rewarding, eventful, and loving life. In no manner could we have foreseen just how worthwhile becoming a part of this community would be. But now, as our walk continues, we know that it has all come to pass.

In 1936, our son Peter joined us, and Phil, our second son, came wide-eyed into the world in August 1939. Just eleven years later, with our private little world startled speechless, Ann suggested that the good Lord had a special postscript for us. And on

14

May 8, 1950, Emmy breezed in and has been breezing ever since. Peter is now an integral part of radio station WJTN in Jamestown, N.Y., where he serves his boss and my close friend, Simon Goldman, as sportscaster–newscaster and also doubles, as he has for every year of their existence, as the play-by-play voice on the stadium public-address system for the Buffalo Bills. We'd like a nickel for every time someone wagered that it was my voice, not Peter's, doing those games. It was Pete's voice—according to the name on the paychecks. Phil has become equally important as a member of the Moog Company staff in East Aurora, N.Y. Both Peter and Phil, during high-school years at Bennett, captained city championship teams and went on to college. Peter graduated in 1958 from Colgate, Phil in 1960 from Duke—the years in which their father attended Poorhouse University.

Emmy, born Emily Louise in honor of my beloved Tem and Ann's blessed mother, Louise, made her contribution to Bennett's athletic prowess by captaining the cheerleading team. She went on to Alfred University, was Homecoming Queen in October of 1971, and graduated in June 1972.

There, then, is my family, and if I moved slightly ahead of myself in the chronicling of events I will retrace my steps and hasten back to February 10, 1935—certainly the red-letter day of a radio career which, to all intents and purposes, actually began at WEBR—as I faced Sam Cordovano, everyone's all-American, on the very first sportscast of my life—a far cry from my poetic beginning. WEBR was in ear-to-ear competition with the two giants of its time, WBEN and the Buffalo Broadcasting Corporation, which comprised WGR and WKBW. Despite their obvious stature, Herbert H. Howell, WEBR's owner, never recognized these two leaders as meaning a thing. He did not believe in ratings, which were practically unheard of then, but he did believe in his station and himself—both of which were also practically unheard of at the time. However, Howell and the late Roy L. Albertson came up with one program entitled "The Town Crier" which not only outstripped anything else in Buffalo but would make mince meat out of the most highly rated radio programs of today. It was a weekly sleeves-rolled-up, invectives-dusted-off, finger-pointed-straight-and-accusingly verbal tirade against any organization, personality, or transaction which Albertson thought was worthy of woodshed consideration. Nothing moved, and I mean nothing, until The Crier, had spilled his dirt on Monday night, and strong men quaked and women swooned and children thought their parents had gone daft.

WEBR had its transmitter in the Larkin Warehouse Building in those years, and the only way you could reach it was via the elevator. Many was the night when law-enforcement officers were sent out to nab Albertson as a result of his vitriolic outbursts, but he foiled all of them by the simple trick of keeping the elevator up and the law down. One of the thrills of my young career was the part that I played each Monday in that most talked about show of them all. At the start of the program, the studio announcer would intone, "Hear ye, hear ye, it is time for 'The Town Crier.' " At the same time, a bell would accompany the pronouncement, and believe it or not I rang the bell.

As 1934 moved into 1935 and the station made its own transition from its second-story shennanigans on Main Street to 23 North Street, another change was taking place—right in back of the middle of my forehead. The BBC was dominant in sports with Roger Baker owning the Bison baseball audience, while WBEN employed a lad named George Sutherland as its sports voice. Sutherland collected more than his share of listeners simply because WBEN was the king of the castle in those years. WEBR had no sports program of any kind mainly because Herb Howell didn't know a foul ball from a bounce pass and couldn't have cared less. So, in my desire to create a sports quarter hour, I had to use a little astuteness. Instead of asking if I could present a sportscast, I told him (during one of the few times he wasn't balling me out), "Mr. Howell, BBC and WBEN are using sports to keep ahead of us." His big neck bulged and his eyes popped because there were two expressions you never, and I mean never, used in his presence:

16

One was WBEN and the other was BBC. As he settled back, breathing heavily, I suggested that, having played a full program of sports in high school myself, I had a working knowledge of them and was keenly interested in trying my hand at such a program.

As recorded here, and many times elsewhere, I began that sportscasting career on the evening of February 10, 1935, in the WEBR studios at 23 North Street—mainly because Herbert H. Howell thought that he had found another way in which to combat the power and the might of WBEN and BBC. It's strange how, even today, I sort of recoil whenever I mention those two in the same sentence with the name of my first radio boss.

Before that first program I spent considerable time in pre-program thinking and preparation. WEBR had no such facilities as wire services, AP or UPI, and couldn't afford the Western Union baseball ticker service. Thus, it was necessary to cull the pages of the three local Buffalo newspapers, *News, Courier* and (the now long gone) *Times,* to find scores—it was all afternoon activity in those years—wherever they could be found or pilfered. Thus, starved for regular, flowing, constant information, it was necessary to develop the guest-interview aspect, and here, again, I was fortunate. A person learns by doing, and through necessity I was forced into interviews and into full original preparation of all scripts from the very moment I started my reporting and editorializing career.

The most wondrous thing that happened to me up to that time came to pass just the day before that initial program. It has always been a special philosophy of mine that it is wise to seek counsel from those who are more mature. Charles Joseph Murray was possibly the best known and most important sports figure in Buffalo then. As a fight promoter, he was famed as the man who brought Jack Dempsey to Buffalo for the first time. He had no peer and not only rubbed elbows with the greatest of the profession, but his wisdom, and cunning were sought by countless other promoters throughout the land. I did not know Charley Murray that day.

17

Yet I sought his counsel because I needed it, and I knew that he would not deny me. Charley answered the phone and I said, "Mr. Murray, tomorrow I am going to start a sports program at 6:15 on WEBR. I'm brand-new and therefore inexperienced and very scared. Could you give me something to hold on to—something out of your life which you think might aid me?" This man, very soon to become my friend, along with John Stiglmeier, not far from becoming a second father, said, simply, "If you can't say something good about a man, don't even mention his name." That became my creed, and I adhered to it throughout my lifetime and it is my creed today.

A second call was placed to Sam Cordovano. Sam was a top-flight wrestler of the day, assistant coach at Columbia under Lou Little, and an all-America footballer while an undergraduate at Georgetown. Today Sam occupies a seat of honor in Georgetown's Sports' Hall of Fame. A big guy, a darling of the gals, and as agile as the Adonis he resembled, not only arrived early but gave a marvelous interview, stayed late, and then wished me well. From time to time he made it a point to see that I met those worth meeting in his realm of sports. Charley Murray did the same thing and so did every person with whom I came in contact.

One day, after the program had been going for a month or so, I passed Mr. Howell's office. He beckoned me, and I walked in. He paid me the finest compliment he could when he said, "We're walking even with those other two, aren't we?" I didn't have to ask him who he meant by "the other two," but I wouldn't have anyway. I'm allergic to being thrown out of offices.

On March, 1936, just a year later, Roy Albertson opened the doors on the sixth floor of the Nellany Building, and at 10:00 A.M. he pressed a button and Buffalo's newest station, WBNY, signalled its way into being. Ironically, Roy Albertson's first two announcers were Jack McLean who befriended me in 1931, and Ralph Hubbell.

4

Radio As It Was

WBNY DIED JUST TWENTY-FIVE YEARS after its inception. However, since I was a part of its cradle years and not present at its death, the whys and wherefores of that demise are not important to our story. The fact that Roy Albertson, one-time secretary to Franklin D. Roosevelt, gave the city another radio station was exceedingly important, though, because WBNY gave me the opportunity to get my full bearings in the realm of radio and in the world of area and national sports. If we were lacking any part of a full sports format at WEBR, the same was not true at the newest peanut whistle on Main Street. Albertson wanted listeners, and he wanted them in any way he could get them, and what better way than to institute an all-out sports program.

During the three years that I was matriculated (I still considered myself an undergraduate at Radio University) at WBNY, I was able to put it all together. We instituted a program which we called "The All Sports Review." It was a two-hour—3 P.M. to 5 P.M.—daily grab bag of music and sports. In relation to other such programs, there was one notable exception—we gave race results from every track in the nation and in Canada, and one of the features of that show was the daily call of a race. This meant that

19

Keyran Hooley, who called the results, would give me the positions of the horses at various stages of the race, and then I would simulate the race, using the crowd sound effects and even the corny sound of flying hooves on occasion. It must have been effective to some extent because a lady came to the studios one day and said that she wanted to watch the race.

Not all of the race calling was good, and some of it was hardly accurate. My most vivid recollection of that program is of a telephone call that I received from a gentleman who was exceedingly polite and very anxious to aid in my beginning, and who suggested that I pay attention to accuracy. It seems that I was sitting back one afternoon, flushed with the success of calling a race with all of our phony frills, when I was told I was wanted on the phone. After a brief greeting, a well-modulated male voice said, "Have you ever actually seen a horse race?" Only slightly taken aback by the certain uneasy feeling that my caller knew darn well I hadn't, I admitted that that part of my education had been neglected. (It should be pointed out right here that I would start a race by glancing at the full field. Then I would mention any of the horses in the contest until an important segment of the race arrived at which time I would start putting the ultimate one, two, and three nags in order. This gave me more of a chance to color the contest and more freedom to mention any horse, listed to start, in the field. But only the theory was good, as we shall see.) My caller, never raising his voice, suggested that, before I call another race, it might be well for me to learn the terminology of horse racing. "For example," he asked, "do you know the definition of the word *scratch?*" "Only as it applies to the human body," I rather facetiously replied. His voice wasn't merry as he said, "In that race you just called you had a horse leading for the entire first half that had been scratched from the race this morning. You take it from there." I thanked him, and the world went on. The next day I sat down with Keyran Hooley, and he gave me a lesson in the terminology of the sport of kings and lucky paupers—horse racing.

In addition to this daily two-hour program, WBNY moved in on the Buffalo Bison baseball broadcasting scene in opposition to BBC, and even if we didn't send the then-titan of baseball description, Roger Baker, to the showers, it was a chance for me to get my feet wet in possibly the most popular sport of that era. Actually, it was invaluable experience, for when I moved on to the BBC in 1939, one of the plusses that aided tremendously in the competitive audition was the fact that I not only knew how to broadcast in-town and out-of-town games, but I was well-indoctrinated in the Bison baseball picture. Along the way, WBNY added Canisius University basketball, and I recall doing some of the old Buffalo Pros games when that ill-fated outfit played in the equally ill-fated but still revered Elmwood Music Hall. If all of it was secondary in listener rating, and I am not certain today that all of it was, it was priceless exposure for me. And, unquestionably, the most absorbing, fascinating, gruelling, and rewarding live sports descriptive work I ever did was to describe the six-day bike-race activities at the old Broadway Auditorium. Before recalling the history of the bike riders, just a passing word concerning that auditorium which was the forerunner to the present magical structure, Memorial Auditorium. Broadway Auditorium was the scene of everything under a roof that was great in sports for many, many years. Amateur boxing (Buffalo having possibly the most solid setup in the world) thrived as the Orioles and the Eagles vied for public favor and found it—each in their own way. When the transition was made, the amateurs lost their way and the pros began to die, too. Only the great dedication of Monsignor Francis Kelleher and his Boys' Town team on Vermont Street had enabled the area to have any boxing at all, and even the good padre will tell you that it is not easy. The professionals—Slats and Rocky Kansas, Jimmy Goodrich, Art Weigand, George Nichols, Mahoney, Clark, DeJohn, Henry Brimm, the Muscatos, Bobby Higgins, and a thousand others—departed without even a service to mark the passing of their careers.

Wrestling was never greater, week after week, than when it

used the Broadway barn for its screeching histrionics, although it is true that men of the magnitude of The French Angel, Gorgeous George, and the rest of that bulging-bicep brigade keep the activity humming in the present-day edifice.

College double-header basketball—joint brainchild of the late Doctor Jim Crowdle of Canisius, and Ned Irish, present president of the NBA New York Knicks—began in that hallowed structure and, with wrestling, moved on to greater heights in Memorial Auditorium.

Six-day bike riding became one of the true sports spectacles of all time and continued up to, but not beyond, the 1938–1939 season. The sport was dependent, almost totally, upon riders from countries other than the United States, and when World War II came along to shatter the universe the riders were called from their play to return to their native lands to learn the techniques of a new game which did not include bicycles. But before they left and took the professional aspect of the great sport of bike riding with them, they gave us enough thrills to last us a lifetime. So vivid are the memories that many times I find myself wishing, against all reason, that the generations which have followed could have been exposed to the daring, the skill, and the drama of those matchless men. One, if he happened to have been there in those years, merely has to close his eyes to see the likes of Letourner, DeBaets, McNamara, Audy, the Walthours, the great Canadian brother team of Torchy and Doug Peden, Tino Reboli, the tireless Teutons, Gus Killian, and Heinz Vopel, Bobby Thomas, and countless others who tirelessly ground each other into the pine saucer which fostered a million splinters, its share of broken bones and pulled muscles, and more than its share of wild acclaim which seemed to greet every moment of every man on the track.

I will never forget Alfie Letourner. Each day's race started at 10 A.M., and the grinding was continuous until 4 A.M.—a total of eighteen hours. The cardinal rule was that no rider could leave the auditorium during the entire week. But Letourner broke the rule six times each week. All doors were barred at 4 A.M. against either going out or coming in. So Letourner, a high-living Frenchman, rose to the challenge—he couldn't have cared less for rules—by going out a window near the roof and then climbing down the wall to the ground. I asked him how he accomplished it and he said, "I will tell you how I get out, but I will never tell anyone how I get back in. You scale a wall down, my friend, you do not scale a wall up." Ah, he was a priceless man and never to be replaced. So, too, was his sport!

There have been many times when I have thought I'd like to write a book devoted entirely to the whirly world of the six-day bike riders. However, let's see how we do with THIS book, first, and maybe one day we'll gather the splinters from the tracks and the arms of the yesterday heros of the pine saucers of the world and let you read as their sprockets turn in memory.

WBNY, in my three years, really came of radio age. Not only was Jack McLean the finest announcer in the entire area, he was a great newsman who worked closely with Walter Fix and Roy Albertson himself. That was a three-way and dynamic news-gathering department which did not require too long to make itself heard in the collective ear of western New York.

About six weeks after WBNY went on the air, a tall, solid, blond individual walked in and asked for an announcing job. His name was, and is, James Gardner Jarrett Wells. Shortly after his arrival at WBNY, he became known to the trade as Jim Wells, and though his fame came later he gave instant notice that a new radio personality was about to literally explode upon our scene. Jim, forming a threesome with McLean and myself, started, as did the rest of us, as a straight announcer. But he had sportscaster written all over his move. And he had a command of the English language that was frightening—he spoke it not only as if he had written it in the first place, but as if he owned it outright. Today, Jim is a World Hockey League executive in Phoenix.

There also was a lad named Jim Britt, who had replaced George Sutherland at WBEN, and Britt, too, was a gifted writer and a talented exponent of the spoken word. The three of us—Wells, Britt, and I—became exceedingly close friends (as did our families) and exceedingly competitive golfers, although I had to make up for my lack of mastery of the ancient and honorable pastime by gently wheedling the necessary strokes from my stingy compatriots on the first tee.

In 1939, the local radio structure submitted to a major transition, and by the time the year was out you couldn't tell the local radio personalities without a scorecard. WBNY and I parted as friends after three irreplaceable years of training and growing, and I moved over to the Buffalo Broadcasting Corporation. This break occurred because Red Barber, the top baseball voice of that era, left Cincinnati to become the voice of the Brooklyn Dodgers, and Roger Baker, the BBC announcer, was selected to take Barber's place. Meanwhile, Jim Britt was summoned to Boston to become the baseball vocal chords of both the Boston Red Sox and the Boston Braves, alternating those teams' home games on The Yankee Network, and my buddy, Jim Wells, was given Britt's spot at WBEN. For the next nine years, Jim at WBEN and I at WGR–WKBW battled each other tooth-and-nail each evening on our respective six 15-minute sports columns. Then, when television arrived on the scene to put radio out of commission, Wells left the field entirely and I assumed command of WBEN.

That television failed in its bid to devastate radio was obvious from the very moment that someone said twenty-four years ago, "When they figure a way to make television workable in an automobile then maybe radio will fade—but until then, T.V. will have to fight for its existence."

5

Change of Address

AS A PREAMBLE TO MY MOVE FROM WBNY to BBC in 1939, let's dwell for a moment on the most fabled sports structure in the long history of Buffalo—Offerman Stadium. The mere mention of this ball park, which before it was hacked apart in the name of progress housed good and great ball players alike, will bring smiles to the faces of those whose haven of baseball it was. For those who deeply resent its razing, to mention Offerman Stadium will cause anger, for, in passing, its destruction brought an end to our beloved sport of professional baseball. Yet Offerman Stadium—home of the Ollie Carnegies, the Beauty McGowans, the Mayo Smiths, the Greg Mulleaveys, the Bucky Crouses, the Fred Hutchinsons, the Johnny Dickshots and Fabian Kowaliks, the Clyde McCulloughs, Virgil Trucks, Bill Harris and Art Houtteman, the Jimmy Hutch's, the Ray Schalks, the Steve O'Neills, the Del Bissonetts, the Gabby Hartnetts, the Bucky Harris's, Mickey Rocco, Smokey Joe Martin, Eddie Boland, Hal White, Paul Richards (or make your own list)—represented Buffalo baseball so completely that not even its physical destruction could possibly erase the memory of its contribution to all the juvenile and adult years of our lives.

No stadium, before, during, or since, boasted of such a

perfectly conditioned infield and outfield as did this one. This was a tribute to the groundskeeping genius of the late Joe Brown, and a further testimonial to his brilliant green thumb. His dedication to his acre of perfection came in the form of yearly visits by groundskeepers from every corner of this nation and Canada. Joe told them all of his secrets, but he saved his green thumb for us. Offerman Stadium was 330 feet down each line and 400 feet to the base of the center-field scoreboard. To ride over the board, a ball had to be hit at least 500 feet. This was accomplished only once, and don't you ever let a soul tell you otherwise. Rumor would have you believe that Ruth, Gehrig, Foxx, Pooch Puccinelli, and a hundred others powered pitches dead center over the board, but its a pack of lies, my hearties, and if you become involved in any discussion concerning who did hit the only one over the big board you tell 'em "Luke Easter hit it, Mister, and only Big Luke." You can wager a hundred to one and win.

In 1936, Offerman Stadium gave me lodgings for the first time. That was the year we won the International League pennant and the play-offs but lost four games to one to Milwaukee in the Little World Series. Buffalo was a great ball club comprised of players who automatically moved into the majors and this was true of all Bison clubs, for our teams gave more greats to the big time than any other minor cities in history. If that's an opinion rather than a fact, it isn't far from being a fact.

The move from WBNY to the BBC, therefore, wasn't of such magnitude, but it represented personal progress and considerably more money. It wasn't as if I had moved from this city to another, for that would have been a major change, and also an impossibility. If you recall, my dedication has always been to this city from the time Ann and I first established residence, and it will remain so throughout the rest of our years. Yes, there were other offers, bigger offers. Yet the only real plus was that we would receive more money. No one could offer us better schools, more or finer friends, a more decent living, or a sounder overall sports structure. We were building where we wanted to build, and we discouraged any suggestions—with thanks, of course—that might force us to leave. We paid rent, so we wouldn't be tossed out, and then we bought a house so that then we couldn't even be evicted.

As I stepped off the elevator that first, official day of my employment at BBC, Ike Lounsberry's bailiwick, I knew that the sequence of my life's events had not been interrupted, for I had been told that an old and trusted friend of mine had decided to make a switch also. So when I spied Jack McLean standing at the reception desk, I walked up, shook his hand, and said; "Isn't this where I came in?" It had been nine years since Jack and I first met and five years since he gave me my first chance. Our relationship was to continue throughout my association with WGR, and today, long since retired, Jack walks quietly, and, I am sure, is secure in the knowledge that at least one individual is deeply grateful to him.

Jealousy was a common emotion among the radio pioneers—the men who were the owners and, therefore, the men who were gambling that the upstart industry would become the bonanza that we all know it to be today. It was jealousy born of fierce, individual pride, and it allowed for no lessening of fierceness in its determination to be better than the next guy. It was what Herb Howell felt in his utter distaste for WBEN and the BBC. It was the same feeling that Roy Albertson had when he turned his back on WEBR to create his own identity at WBNY. In 1936 he disclaimed all loyalty to WEBR, which he had served as general manager, and he developed a new resentment for WBEN and the BBC simply because he was in a hard business.

The man at the helm of my new organization, Ike Lounsberry, was as jealous as the rest, I suppose, but he was a fair man in every regard and wise enough to know that WGR and WKBW, ran second and third best to WBEN, which enjoyed a stature in those years that seemed destined to insure its dominance of the local radio scene for all time to come. It is of no consequence to this saga that that impression is now a thing of the past. The fact that others, never yielding in their desire to improve, have cut deeply into the

27

prestige of WBEN is only natural, but Ike Lounsberry was possibly the most astute executive in local radio annals. He built a powerful organization at WGR–WKBW, and when the Federal Communications Commission forced the two stations to go separate ways, Ike stayed with WGR and made it a fine major-league operation. For me, it was a thrill just to be associated with the station and with Lounsberry and with the hundreds of guys and dolls with whom I worked through those nine eventful years.

6

Those Fabulous Forties

THE START OF THE 1940s HERALDED A DEC-ade of athletic activity that made Buffalo one of the hotbed sports cities in the nation. It was then that the Buffalo Hockey Club, in the American League, opened shop, with the great goalie of Ranger years, Tiny Thompson, as its first coach. In that same era, Buffalo Raceway and Batavia Downs swung wide their standardbred track doors.

In 1945, Sam Cordovano asked me if I could arrange a meeting with a wealthy oil man by the name of Jim Breuill. At the time I was sponsored by Breuill's Frontier Oil Company, so such arranging was easy. At a luncheon in the Buffalo Athletic Club, Breuill and Cordovano agreed on the formation of a professional football team to compete in a new loop, the All American Conference. The following year the Buffalo Bills came into existence, and for the next four years—the life span of the AAC—some areas that had no exposure to the long-dominating titan, the National Football League, had a chance to see the sport and root for the homebreds. And it was tremendous football. The Cleveland Browns, so star-studded that they strangled the conference, moved from a dead loop in 1950 and answered all of the critics by walking into the National Football League and treating the league's very best with such little respect that the NFL went and hid in shame. Ah, but that was a club.

Football's history book is filled with the exploits of the Cleveland Browns. Strong memory respects that team of the AAC years and the Browns' own beginning years in the NFL as one of the most awesome machines that ever ground out yardage or flew on the wing of the legendary Otto Graham. Marion Motley, Mac Speedie, Dante Lavelli, Lou Saban, Lou Groza, Horace Gillom, and the legion of troops under their supreme commander, Paul Brown, formed a football dynasty that earned the respect of all football men wherever the game was played and in some spots of the world where it was only hearsay. But, in leaving the conference after 1949, Cleveland devastated that which it had left behind. The All American Conference simply died, with no memorial services, and although a superlative effort was made here in town to save the Bills, they faded from view. It was a long and miserable ten years from 1950 to 1960 when about the only thing that happened to Civic Stadium, where football was played, was a change in its name to War Memorial Stadium.

If football was to start and quickly die here, at least the same fate was not in store for the hockey forces. The organization started strong in the 1940–1941 season, was given the blessing and the genius of Eddie Shore two years later, and went on to become the finest franchise away from the NHL, thanks to the good fortune that prompted the Pastor brothers (Reuben, Sam, and Abraham) to cast their lot with us in the mid-fifties. The Pepsi generation, which was the proud product represented by the Pastors, became the hockey generation until the year 1969. The sport had simply become too big for its minor-league boots in western New York, and the Pastors sold to the Knoxes who paid dearly for the privilege of establishing an expansion club here in the National Hockey League.

My life was deeply affected by the advent of the Buffalo Bills. It added another dimension to the reporting career of any sportscaster or writer, and during the four years that the club operated it was my Sunday task to call the plays on the stadium public-address system. As was noted earlier, my son Peter called them for the present-day Bills, so, in the total of seventeen years that the old and the new pro footballers were losing more than they were winning in the old stadium, the Hubbells went seventeen for seventeen in the matter of yearly play calling.

The hockey situation was an even greater plus for me because it gave me the opportunity to broadcast the activities of the team for ten years. Those were exciting and action-filled years, and I am grateful for them if only because they brought me into contact with Frederick Tennyson Hunt, the poet of the ice, and the man most important to Buffalo hockey from its very inception to this very day.

Freddy Hunt, a graduate of St. Michael's College in Toronto, was one of the greatest professional softball players in Canada's history. But a guy doesn't get rich pitching an underhanded, oversized ball no matter how great he happens to be. Hunt was a star collegiate hockey player, and when the time came he traded in his smaller amateur checks for the larger pro stipends in order to make a decent buck, and therefore a decent living. Freddy had a short bout in the NHL, but he had a fabled career in the American Hockey League. And he arrived in Buffalo by chance. When the war came, Eddie Shore's Springfield franchise had to either find another place to play or suspend for the duration. Shore, rated one of the finest of all major-league defensemen, wasn't one to just sit back because of a slight disturbance. True, his building in Springfield had been taken over by the War Department, but, as with all things, there is more than one way to beat any rap.

So Eddie Shore made a deal with Buffalo. He would blend his franchise with ours (meaning his players with ours) and operate out of Buffalo for the duration. And that is what came to pass, and the result of that was possibly the finest organization in hockey history. Shore came to Buffalo as general manager, and while he was at the helm this was the city where you lived if you wanted to see a club win. Fred Hunt was a player for Shore, and that is how the diminutive master of back checking became a Buffalonian. Except for a very brief stint with the Hershey Bears, Hunt was here to

31

stay. First a player and then a coach, Freddy moved into the general manager position and served Bison hockey for eighteen consecutive years in that capacity. When the clan Knox took over and established the Sabres for the NHL, they recognized the true ability of Hunt and installed him as assistant general manager to the storied Punch Imlach, who also served as coach until he was temporarily felled by a heart attack in 1972. Imlach's old pal, Joe Crozier, was summoned from the Sabre farm club in Cincinnati to become interim coach. Then, in a decree that came close to breaking Imlach's heart, which had trouble enough, his doctors told Punch he would have to quit coaching and continue only as general manager. Thus Joe Crozier was given the post, listening closely to the counsel of Imlach, and Hunt became a more vital factor than ever in his relations with the team.

There is no question about the fantastic contribution made to the city of Buffalo by the Knox family. They are one of Buffalo's oldest, and most social and philanthropic dynasties, and the impact of this contribution is too staggering to even comprehend. Witness the spending of millions of dollars to establish Buffalo as the hockey center of the nation in much the same manner as the elder Seymour Knox has with his insatiable devotion to art, created a lasting tribute to his family and to this city with Albright Knox Art Galleries. Seymour and his brother, Northrup, are the men, along with David Forman, who are the executive heads of the Sabres. If it is going to be a long, hot spell before Buffalo comes out a hockey winner in this dog-eat-dog sport, though it may be shorter than most believe, you can be sure that Buffalo will not fail. Not as long as these three men have the dedication to give of themselves the wisdom to be patient, and the money to burn. Except that rich men don't burn money—that's for the paupers.

During the hockey broadcasting years in the AHL, I worked from a rink corner section of the red seats in the auditorium; those were the comfortable years when an announcer worked alone. I always subscribed to one announcer doing the play-by-play along with the integrated color commentary, while a second announcer handled the commercials. This is in contrast to today when there is

32

such an effort to field an announcing team that the game being depicted is secondary to all of the comments, the cross comments, the endless statistics, and the constant attempt at humor. However, if it gives more guys work, then I'm for it, and when you come right down to it, I don't have to worry about it anymore. As one man said to me once: "The nice thing about your work is that, if I don't like it, I can just flip a button."

One of the stories I will always remember had to do with a fellow by the name of Jimmy Dray. Dray, well-known in Buffalo for being a tremendous hockey fan as well as a tremendous guy and good golfer, was the vocal kind of enthusiast. Thus, when he attended a game—and I don't recall that he ever missed a Bison game—he would bring a small, Rudy Vallee-type megaphone and Jimmy had the built-in human battery to make it work for sixty minutes of every hour's game. He rested only between periods. Jimmy's main target was a Hershey defenseman by the name of Billy Moe. This individual was not only a fine defenseman, but also a mixture of Ray Robinson's skill and Hank Armstrong's pistonlike power. He loved nothing more dearly, than mixing with one of the enemy, and all men outside a Hershey uniform were Billy Moe's enemies.

Dray and Moe were from worlds apart except when the Bears were in town. The minute Billy would step on the ice, Jimmy started; and when the final buzzer sounded, Jimmy stopped—never, mind you, in between. And Moe was always aware of the presence of his tormentor. One night, in Cleveland, Moe suffered a pulled muscle. Thus, when the team moved on to Buffalo for a game the next night, Billy came but didn't dress. So, diabolically, I went to the Hershey dressing room before the game and asked Moe if he would be my guest between periods. He was agreeable. Then I went to Dray and asked him, inasmuch as he was now famous and had never been interviewed, if he would be my guest between periods. He was delighted, he said. So I went back, called the first period, and then sat back awaiting the drama which was only seconds away. Dray made his way from his seat from one side of the auditorium, while Moe came up from the dressing room

33

from the other side. Thus they did not see each other until they came face to face at our microphone. By some strange quirk Dray was clutching his megaphone, and when they confronted each other each knew immediately who the other guy was. The looks on their faces were absolutely classic.

As the interview started, the fans in their seats watched and suddenly sensed what was happening. What started as a ripple of booing exploded into one thunderous boo, and to this day I don't believe that either man has ever forgotten the incident. And it is a matter of record that every time Moe appeared here from then on, every seat was sold except one. That was Jimmy Dray's—the club gave it to him as a bonus.

The forties had to be the most important years in my career. Not only was I afforded the chance of broadcasting everything in sight, but I had the rare opportunity to work with top men and women in the still fairly new field of radio. And to work in competition with those who made Buffalo's brigade of sportscasters as great a collective bunch as there were in any other place in the United States. Jim Britt had left when the forties hit, but Jim Wells stayed. Van Patrick, who became one of Detroit's most distinguished sports announcers, was in action here both at WEBR and WBEN before heading to the Midwest to announce the Notre Dame Fighting Irish and the Detroit Lions. His death was felt wherever games were played. Bill Mazer came as the 1940s concluded, and had a fine career here (he was matchless calling a basketball game) before he moved to New York and the new worlds he conquered.

Of those who were outstanding here but who didn't get away, there was Charlie Bailey, who doubled in brass as an all-around sportscaster and sports columnist with the *Courier Express;* Sieg Smith, who left the field and today is secretary to a U.S. Senator in Washington, D.C.; Bob Kliment, today a radio executive here in town; and other lesser lights, who made their contributions and then pulled up stakes.

7

Escape from March

NINETEEN THIRTY-NINE WAS MY FIRST
year at WGR and my first year covering spring training in Florida
with the Buffalo club. That year the Bisons worked hand in glove
with the Indians of Cleveland, as Steve O'Neill directed the
fortunes of the Buffalo teams. First impressions never really leave
a person's system, I am sure, and my first impression of spring
training, a beat that every kid would give both arms and a leg to
cover, was that this was a never-never land of make-believe. In
1939, we trained in Plant City, Florida, which was famed for
Tony Mike's bar and the fact, according to the boast, that Plant
City was the strawberry center of the world. It could have been,
but they give me a rash, so I never actually found out.

One morning—as scared as the rawest rookie, being a raw
rookie myself—as I ate an early breakfast alone in a restaurant, a
couple of equally timid souls walked in and came over and sat with
me. One of them said, "You play baseball?" I admitted that I
didn't but that I was in truth a sportscaster from Buffalo covering
the club. Then the other one said, "Do they travel in buses in this
league?" I said, "Nope, they travel in trains." They ordered
something to eat and admitted that they were both scared and that
this was their first venture to a top minor-league training camp.

35

After breakfast we walked out to the ball park together, and having found strength in each other's admitted butterflies we were friends. One was a kid aspiring to play second base by the name of Ray Mack. The other was a guy from the University of Illinois who fancied himself as a shortstop; his name was Lou Boudreau. One year later they were the talk of the baseball world with the Cleveland Indians, and the rest is baseball history. In their very first year they developed a never-before-seen defensive play in which Boudreau would dart back of second, scoop up a ground ball, toss it back to Mack, and Ray would get the man at first. No, they didn't travel by bus—they went first class as becomes class men.

That same first spring, Jim Wells, now Public Relations Chief of the Phoenix Hockey Club, which is a member of the World Hockey League, was down there covering the training for WBEN. Being buddies for many years, we naturally were sidekicks in Florida and well do I recall a day when Buffalo had a game to play against the Newark Bears in Sebring. We arose very early and beat the crew to Sebring so as to be able to play a round of golf before we had to cover the game. We had all of the correct gear, and we clutched a couple of PGA cards which were invaluable because they not only entitled us to play any affiliated course in Florida, but they enabled us to play for nothing. And though we were on expense accounts that was good news. When we walked into the pro shop, we were dressed to a tee and ready for the wars. There were a few hangers-on sitting around, and when we hauled out those cards they figured we were pros. So when we sauntered to the first tee, they strolled out to watch us tee off.

Wells hooked his into the oranges on the left, and I sliced mine into the grapefruit on the right. After that one look, the hangers-on went back to their business of hanging on. We had a caddy who must have been seventy-five and thrice as wise. When I went into the grove and found my ball, I noticed a small sign that told me I could drop onto the fairway with only a one-stroke penalty. But there was no chicken in me, so I took out an iron and prepared to carve my way out of the sand. With a debonair, "Well, the Lord hates a coward," I started my preliminary stroke. With a tired, wise word of bored counsel which bespoke a century of patience, my caddy said, "He also hates a fool." It was the only time I was ever able to actually halt a golf swing on its downward flight.

At training camp in 1941, Wells and I considered ourselves old hands, and we had a pretty fair circle of friends native to Florida who resided in the unthriving and unhumming community of Plant City. That spring of 1941 was to be our last in Plant City, and though our move to Fort Pierce, on the east coast, was considered a step up, not one of us ever forgot the city of strawberries if only because, for many of us, it marked our baptismal location for induction into the wonders of being in Florida while there was still snow on the ground back home.

That spring a lad by the name of Mayo Smith was traded to Buffalo from Toronto, and for the next five years there was no more agile, perceptive center fielder in the International League. His pal was Greg Mulleavey, storied Buffalo shortstop, who was a year away from player retirement and a brief run at managing. When free time was ours for the taking, it just seemed sort of natural to have Smith and Mulleavey team up against Wells and Hubbell in whatever little game of skill and chance happened our way. One particular day, a most unusual one, all hands had a full day off and our fearless foursome seized upon the chance to go at our friendly competition with no time elements involved. We played a round of golf, and Mayo and Greg gave us a good, real good, trouncing. Then we repaired to a miniature course, and there, on the final stroke of the entire match, Smith holed out to whip us again. The jut-jawed Wells hated the idea of losing with a vengeance. Thus two defeats in one day, at the hands of our arch rivals, ignited his normally short fuse in less time than usual. He looked the enemy in the eyes and said, "All right, let's play *my* game." Smith looked at Mulleavey and I looked at Jim and everyone chorused, "What *is* your game?" Wells almost screamed it: "It's pool—that's what my game is." So we repaired to the only billiard establishment in Plant City and set our mind to playing Jim's game.

The privilege of breaking the balls fell to me. Mulleavey then followed and managed a ball or two, and when he missed, it was Wells's turn at the table. Say it for Jim, he knew which end of the cue to point at the cue ball, and he proved he was no novice by eliminating nine of the balls without drawing a deep breath. Then he missed and that, dear friends, was the last mistake that was made during that pool match that afternoon in Plant City, Florida, strawberry center of the world. No one told Jim, Greg Mulleavey or me that Mayo Smith had not only played the game before that fatal afternoon but when he was fourteen he was known as the boy wonder of Florida pool halls.

Smith, who later came to baseball prominence as the manager of the Cincinnati Reds and the Detroit Tigers, ran the required number of balls to total the fifty which we had agreed upon as the victory total. As the cue ball clicked its precisionlike cadence over and over again, Jim's face was a study of controlled frustration, anger, and despair. Finally, and with an uncontrolled explosion that was unmistakable to the naked ear, Wells bolted out of the front door after sailing his cue toward the rack. And he never looked back. It's just as well, for such a glance would have revealed Mr. Smith doubled in two in convulsive laughter. For some strange reason, that incident was never referred to in the presence of the aforementioned Jim Wells. For it was the greatest—or the most heartbreaking extra-curricular defeat of his life.

No flashback to spring training would ever be complete if it failed to include those precious memories of the fabled Jimmy Oates, the Irish thrush, who ran an Allen Street pub in Buffalo for many, many years. Jimmy started as a singing waiter, and his voice, so crystal clear and true that you were sure it must be a fantasy, long outlived his table-waiting days and his slim physique.

38

Jimmy was corpulent, about five feet five inches tall, had hair which seemed spun from silver, and if the devil didn't live in Jimmy's eyes, he sent the impish sparkle to him as a gift. For Oates was the master imp of all time. In spring of 1946, when things were getting back to normal and baseball had gone back to Florida again, Oates announced to me one day that he was going with me to Winter Haven. That was our training base that year, and it marked the first of many junkets that Oates and I embarked upon together. We took my car for two reasons: first, Oates didn't have a car, and second Oates didn't know how to drive. But he loved to ride. He'd plant that rotund body of his in the back seat and then would literally be chauffeured to Florida.

That first year we hit Georgia as dawn broke on St. Patrick's Day. That was a signal for Jimmy to observe the greatest day of the Irish calendar, and he did it in the only way he knew how—he sang his way through Georgia. About midmorning Oates was looking for something to ease that dry feeling in his throat. Not booze, mind you. That had come the night before, and Jimmy had one theory about drinking that he always adhered to: Never drink on the second day. Being my copilot as we chugged along that red clay highway, Oates suddenly beeped; "There's a little store." I stopped the car, and Jim got out of the back seat (sometimes it required a shoehorn) and ambled up the steps. He wished the dumbstruck inmates a happy St. Patrick's Day and then he said, "Because you have this lovely garden spot which greets two men as a desert oasis gives fanciful succor to a parched throat, I am going to sing for you." The storekeeper just looked blank. Then Oates began to sing right out on the porch. He sang for one solid hour, and he sang every Irish song that was ever written and a couple, I am sure, that he made up that day. He churned that red-clay countryside into Kelly green Irish grass, and he made the skies ring with the glories of Ould Ireland. And you can accept it from me as gospel, friends, that when the concert ended there were over five hundred people who had come, as if produced by sleight-of-hand, from all around the area. It took a good fifteen minutes to wedge Oates back into the car because the Georgians had come to love this leprechaun and they intended to keep him for their very own. Just when I thought that they would succeed, Oates blurted out, "Drive, you dumb fool, and let's get out of here." We made it, but just by the width of the Blarney stone.

8

A Crisis—and Triumph

UP TO THIS JUNCTURE IN THE HUBBELL fortunes the tenor of our ways was pretty even. Then, in 1966, so much happened that just the sorting out of events, in itself, becomes a rather monstrous proposition.

What I am about to reveal is done so with the full knowledge that no life can be completely lived without its share of failure, frustration, heartbreak, self analysis, and, with a gladsome heart do I say it, ultimate and conclusive victory. Both Ann and I experienced each of these emotions separately, as well as together, but they began with me.

Any person who has been under the gun of public observation for a long period of time knows that when you are taken into the bosom of any gathering you are subjected to the rigors of temptation—there is no reason to beat around the bush because there is no shame in this. Plainly and simply, drinking the drinks that were forever being sent my way became a natural thing. Never did I miss a broadcast nor was I ever involved in any unpleasantness because of my penchant for more than an isolated martini, but as the days moved along I could sense that something was happening. My writing was beginning to come grudgingly and there was no flow to it.

41

When worry set in, I realized that it was time to take a look at myself. So I terminated my association with WBEN after eighteen wonderful years and simply walked away. When you do not think that drinking affects you, you are inclined to mediate your case in favor of yourself by saying that drinking is just a way of easing tensions. When I left WBEN, I stayed with the martinis while I spent some time working as host in a restaurant. I also started doing public relations work for the Ontario Jockey Club and began to write a weekly column, "The Human Side," for the *Magnificat,* the western New York Diocesan paper.

In 1966, the Jockey Club, Ltd., of Ontario—now the Ontario Jockey Club—offered me a post in public relations representing that organization in Western New York. Today this relationship with Pres. John Mooney and his magical crew is a deep rooted and wonderful one. Things were proceeding away from my chosen radio and TV career, and people were simply unbelievably good to me. But I still hadn't been able to get to a green olive first without draining off the fluid.

In January 1967, Ann was laid low and hospitalized. It was on February 8, 1967, with Ann still recuperating in the hospital that, out of the darkness of the night, I walked into the sunlight.

Jean and Chuck Healy had asked me over for dinner, and after a cordial I said my thanks and went around the corner to the house on Huntington. As I walked into the living room, I was amazed to find Emmy, who should have been in bed, Peter, who should have been in Batavia where he worked, and Phil, who should have been home with his family. Only Merry Christmas, our mostly Beagle, should have been there to greet me.

As if someone had spilled a glass of cold water over my head, I realized that this was no ordinary gathering of Ann's and my beloved progeny. This was for all of the marbles, and in an attempt at bravado I said, "What's this—a council of war?" It fell flat against the walls. Peter and Phil were dead serious, and Emmy looked as if she would cry. Merry Christmas slept through it all. Phil said, "Dad, we would like to talk to you." Wisely, Dad said nothing. Phil said, "We think we are a wonderful family, and we know that you and Mom have given us everything possible to make our lives happy and complete. Now we want to ask you to promise us that as long as you live you will never take another drink."

Slowly I looked at each of my children and said, "I promise." Emmy went to bed so relieved by the adjournment that she just belted up the stairs. Peter and Phil looked at me, smiled, and without a word walked out the door, to their cars and to their families. What did I do? Well, I stood there for a long minute trying to realize that I had made a promise that must be kept, and then I put out the lights and started up to bed. As I walked up those stairs I recall thinking, "How do you know you can keep that promise?"

As if Someone unseen had been in on the summit meeting the night before, when I awoke the next morning I knew that I would never take another drink as long as I lived. And you can know that I haven't. What was most marvelous was that I never felt the need for another drink—all I really needed was to take the step and stop. And for that I needed my very own kids to shake me free. But the road back was just starting. For two weeks later—a two-week period which the doctors claimed saved my life—every day that I arose to get dressed, and as I prepared to shave, I thought I was in an Oriental bathroom—I was yellowed from my scalp to my toes. That night, as Ann came home from her hospitalization, I moved into another hospital, and after forty days and forty nights of touch and go my rehabilitation from cirrhosis of the liver began.

We never looked back once. It became evident that we had been spared to live on. You may wonder at my telling you this infinitely private story of my children's confrontation with me. Let me quickly set your minds straight. If our story can help only one person, we want it told. Many times since then people have called me or written to me, and I have been able to counsel them. My hope is that we were able to help in some way. My belief is that we were.

43

Throughout the ordeal, the Jockey Club and the *Catholic News* people were simply astounding in their faith and their belief in me. The ravages of such a malady as was designated for me to whip are deep and destructive. The big challenge now became working full-time with the Ontario Jockey Club, doing every form of publicity and public relations function. And I feel certain that you will enjoy meeting that family and of learning how, in 1966, it all came about in the first place.

The phone rang one morning, and Charley Bailey was at the other end. It seems that as each word follows in the spelling out of my life, Bailey keeps reminding me of how important he has been as a friend down through the years. Newspaper writer and later sportscaster, Bailey rated as tops in both fields. Charley asked how things were going and suggested that I might like to look into the possibility of doing some public relations work with the Ontario Jockey Club. Quite naturally, during my reporting years I had had much contact with this organization which took over the Fort Erie racetrack in the mid-fifties and which, in its attentiveness to progress, has created one of the most distinguished track operations in the world. The OJC embraces thoroughbred activity at Fort Erie, as well as Woodbine and Greenwood—both tracks skirting the home of the Royal York, Toronto. The OJC also conducts standardbred (trotters and pacers) activities at Garden City in St. Catherines, Ontario, Mohawk Raceway in Campbleville, Ontario, and at Greenwood in Toronto's backyard.

The old saw about truth being stranger than fiction never found a more credible ally than in the sport of horse racing. Through my years of association with the OJC I have heard so many tales of woe, that I marvel that people can keep coming back for more punishment day after frustrating day. At one time, as a sort of defensive measure, I thought of spending my racing hours on the backstretch, away from the sorrowing throng. But I was certain that even there, in a hideaway haven, some nag would go by me and hand me one of his celebrated grins which would say louder than words, "So you got hooked on the horses through your friends who got hooked by us too."

There are thousands of great horse stories that I could tell you, but I'll limit myself to just one—my favorite. It seems that during the Dunnigan years at Hamburg there was a fine horse by the name of Captain Cash. He was very much to my liking, so I headed down to wager two dollars across, win, place, show, on the Captain to command the field. But when I arrived, my horse was an odds-on favorite at 2 to 5. What kind of gamble is that? As I neared the window and was about to pull out of the line, the man in front of me said, "Let me have number 8." So, for no reason, I said, in identical tones, "Let me have number 8." When I turned and looked at the board in the infield, number 8 was 70 to 1, and I was so taken aback that I refused to return to the press box and confess my foolish change of heart to my confreres. I went high up in the grandstand to watch the race. Number 8 was a nag who looked like a parcel of bones toting a brown coat and a buggy. The name, in case you need an introduction, was Ring Up Seniah, and as I looked at him and as I watched him leave the starting gate I figured that a better name for him would be "Mr. Thousand to Nothing."

Ring Up Seniah was dead last halfway through the backstretch, and as they hit the far turn and headed for the last bit of ribboned track toward the wire he was still last. Then, with my heart trying an escape act from my chest, that old codger was moved to the outside and he finished first by three lengths. And he returned, across the board, $150.00 to win, $33.00 to place, and $13.00 to show!

The final note relative to the Ontario Jockey Club must, in the name of truth alone, be a personal thank you and a respectful tribute to its president, John J. Mooney. It was this man, born to the sport of racing, more than any other man, who by his vision, his loyalty, and his inherent ability, brought the OJC into the sun and kept it shining as he has kept it growing. The Ontario Jockey

Club took over the run down and antiquated Fort Erie racetrack during the mid-fifties, and from that moment until today, with Mooney the master architect and E. P. Taylor, one of Canada's most distinguished individuals, footing the bills, this organization has known only continual growth. No phase of racing has been overlooked in Mooney's zeal and his promise that one day, and in the not too distant future, there will be no more respected racing organization in the world than the Ontario Jockey Club.

That's why it is such a joy and a pleasure to be the American arm, at least up to the elbow, of the OJC. My function is to preach the gospel of Fort Erie and Garden City, the standardbred track in St. Catherines, to the folks in our country who are within easy shouting distance of Canada. Continuous public-speaking appearances throughout the area enable me to keep contacts I established through the years. More than that, we have worked out special group programs for all organizations—and it is an easy sell, believe me. Canada is a courteous country, and its residents are, in truth, good neighbors of ours. This must reflect those who administered that nation in a very glowing light just as it reflects John Mooney and his staff, the lifeblood of the OJC, in as warming a concept. Mooney is the man, no mistaking that, and he is no come-lately to the racing scene. His father, J. D. Mooney, was one of Canada's finest jockeys and one of only four hardboots in all of racing's history to win both the Kentucky Derby and the Queen's Plate—top-quality races in the U.S. and Canada, respectively. The son simply took it from his father's stirrups. How far he will ultimately take it is an unanswerable question, but for certain John Mooney will never rest until he commands the finest racing organization in the world. And he's gaining with each furlong.

9

The Home Teams

THE BILLS

THE MAN CAME HERE FROM DETROIT. HE was a successful man because he not only had a basic business know-how but was a wise investor. When this man from Detroit, Ralph Wilson by name, announced in 1959 that he was signing a deal which would establish a franchise for Buffalo in the new American Football League, there were fears expressed for his mental balance. Those fears were not groundless since Buffalo, which watched its Bills die with the All American Conference, had hit upon evil sports days. There was no college football here except for the University of Buffalo, but, though good, this team hardly satisfied those thousands of non-UB alumni who wanted to root for a team of vital interest to themselves. Professional baseball was beginning to come apart at the seams after a tough battle to achieve major status in the sixties failed. Basketball and hockey were sound, but hockey was years away from major status, as was basketball, professionally speaking.

The question concerning Buffalonians was whether Wilson, an outsider, could come into this camp and restore a football situation that had died ten years earlier. Yet Ralph Wilson not only believed in himself but developed, after a close look at the record of support given the original Bills by area fans, a deep-rooted faith in this territory. While all Buffalo interests continued to ignore the chance to reestablish western New York as a major pro-sports entity, Wilson picked up his fat wallet and proved his faith by bringing to town as much hope as promise. That Wilson had studied well, that he had been correct in assuming that fan reaction would be instantaneous, was immediately reflected in 1960 when the Bills went off to battle for the first time. War Memorial Stadium was jumping that day as it has jumped ever since and that includes the 1971–1972 season, when the Bills won only a single game out of fourteen league encounters played. Buffalo and area fans were starved for major sports activity, and Ralph Wilson knew it and acted when the time was absolutely right.

The Bills, as all teams must, experienced their growing pains. After three years, orderliness and experience infiltrated the organization, and the growing began to manifest itself. When Lou Saban, the same guy who had been such a dominant force as a player with the Cleveland Browns, came upon the scene, he brought with him his needle for the express purpose of injecting new life and fiery new dedication and inspiration into the young team that was beginning to show definite signs of coming of age.

Saban and the Bills owned the mid-sixties in the American League. Lou, as head coach, developed one of the most awesome defensive lines in the entire history of the game, and when he and Jack Kemp throwing and Cookie Gilchrist—the cookie that never crumbled—running or blocking for other runners or pass protecting for Kemp, he had a team that simply mopped up.

Wilson, Saban, Gilchrist, and Kemp, as well as scores of other ball players in a never-ending show of strength, were the key men as Buffalo came of football age for a second time around. And there was one other man who must never be allowed even a second of neglect when reconstructing the past, for it well may be that his contribution, his brilliant perceptiveness, and his administrative know-how combined to make him the single individual who jelled the entire situation. When he followed Saban out the exit door, the

Bills, as an American Football League power were diluted to rather pathetic also-rans.

His name is Dick Gallagher and he's famous today because he deals in that commodity: fame. Gallagher departed our limits to accept an offer to head up the Football Hall of Fame in Canton, Ohio. In the few, extremely short years since Dick assumed command of that shrine of the pro aspect of the game, it has come to its full stature.

Gallagher received his indoctrination during his years in Cleveland with Paul Brown. To learn under Brown, as to learn hockey under Eddie Shore and baseball under Joe McCarthy, was tantamount to learning English at Oxford. There simply never has been a better teacher, and after a close, rewarding association with his pupil I have a hunch that there never was a better student than Dick Gallagher. Gallagher's job here was to evaluate the talent and to work closely with Saban, an old friend, in the careful integration of the talent with the system. After winning consecutive AFL titles in 1964 and 1965, the Saban/Gallagher partnership was broken and so was the magic of the Bills.

Just before we head into the last quarter, I'd like to clear up one point that became of national importance during the mid-sixties. Buffalo, as the world knows, had quarterback Jack Kemp. Jack had been taken in trade from San Diego, and it was quite a tribute to Kemp, at least a tribute to his potential, because at the time he had a broken finger on his pitching hand. Buffalo also had a young fellow with all the world in front of him by the name of Daryle Lamonica, who, whenever the situation warranted, would replace Kemp. One season Lamonica was given credit for some six wins after taking over for the sometimes erratic veteran.

The situation began to pall on Lamonica. One day, when we were at the airport heading for a game in New York, he was particularly glum. I asked him what his problem was and he said, "My idea of professional football is to play it and not stand around in the wings waiting for another guy to make a mistake. And I'm going to do something about it." What Daryle did was to tell the

49

Bills that either he wanted to be traded or he would quit the game. That was fair enough. After all, it was his life. But it posed quite a problem for Saban because he knew that Daryle would make it big one day but that he was winning with Kemp who was an exceptionally inspirational quarterback and that's what a pro club needs more than anything else. A little inspiration can compensate for a whole parcel of errant passes. So Lou made the logical move, and Lamonica wound up in Oakland.

The following years the Bills began to fade, even with Kemp, whereas the Raiders started to gain prominence, with Lamonica leading the way. What made it so difficult on the local scene was that, invariably, after the Bills had gone down to defeat, the fans would hurry home and watch the late afternoon game on TV to see Oakland winning, with Lamonica on the mound, just about every Sunday. This merely added fuel to an already burning controversy which centered around keeping Kemp and allowing Lamonica to get away. But the Bills couldn't keep them both, as a team can have only one starting quarterback; that is, only one man who is number one. Saban definitely made the wiser choice—and if you don't believe me, ask Daryle Lamonica.

The Bills situation began to deteriorate when owner Ralph Wilson made a grave mistake in not granting Coach Saban a two-year contract when it came time to talk turkey again. Under this man the Bills had come to national prominence and a position of dignity in the realm of professional football, and the franchise had become of great value. Yet when Saban, whose genius had jelled all of the necessary parts into a cohesion that few teams have ever experienced, sought security, he was denied more than a one-year parchment. Lou Saban, and justly so, packed his gear and journeyed on to the University of Maryland, an ill-fated stop-off along his way, and thence to Denver and a return to the American League.

Saban's departure definitely marked the start of the long drought which, ironically, won't end until Lou Saban, himself, ends it. For the creator of Buffalo as a football power is back at the helm here in Billville, and you can be sure he returned on *his* terms and not those of Ralph Wilson. Lou will be here for awhile—his contract notes that as fact. During Saban's absence Wilson changed coaches more quickly than John Havlicek moves toward a Celtic basket. Twice, in the post-Saban years, did the owner attempt to install Harvey Johnson as head coach—and twice did the experiment fail. Johnson is the Bill's personnel director, and upon each occasion when his boss told him to call the shots he let it be known that he was unhappy—plenty unhappy. Surrounding these abortive attempts at establishing one man to get the job done on a permanent basis were tenures held by Joel Collier, who had been Saban's top assistant here and who later followed him to Denver, and John Rauch, who, after a great career with Oakland, was brought in, handed a four-year contract, and then was fired halfway through the contract, before part of his teachings could bear fruit. Harried Harvey Johnson had to take the 1971 weekly shellackings, and when the situation became truely alarming, Wilson went back to the man who had created the miracle in the first place—Lou Saban.

Throughout all of this mediocrity and sorry displaying of temperaments, one thing did not change and will never change. The attitude of the fans in this area has been, is now, and will ever be: We want a professional ball team to call our own, and we will stay with it as long as a team plays here. It suggested many times that Ralph Wilson move his franchise but Wilson came here believing in the fans and, if other facets of the operation failed from time to time, no part of the fan loyalty ever showed any semblance of weakening. The fans came to look at the beginning, remained to cheer during the brief glory years, and remain to fight back with the Bills now that the evil days have clutched the area by the throat.

The return of Saban has everyone agog because football in Buffalo has and will continue to have a gridiron winner again. His tremendous football acumen and his attitude in dealing with younger men are characteristics which have been stocks-in-trade of other coaches as well as the Bills' mentor. However, he has a most priceless asset that sets him apart from the others—and that is

51

patience. It is his knack of making time, a precious ally if used correctly, work for him. It is his attitude of being willing to suffer and learn before he expects the world to crumble at his feet. Lou Saban built a citadel of football strength once before, and he will come back into the sun again.

The backdrop for the road back to football prominence is magnificent Rich Stadium which, in its 1973 debut, played to 90 percent capacity and which, in 1974, could easily go the full 100 percent in light of the lightning-like change of football fortunes effected by Lou Saban and company. After one year of experimentation in which Saban used a brand-new broom to sweep his locker room clean, the Buffalo Bills suddenly came of age to the point where, not expected to break even, they finished with a record of nine victories and five defeats—and missed a play-off position by the width of a football.

Architect Saban, with the youngest-age-per-player average in all of professional football, built his club around two-purpose O. J. Simpson. The coach knew he had the greatest running back in the game, but he knew also, that he had a man who could be the spiritual, emotional, inspirational leader of the club. "But," as Lou explained to me, "my first job is to make O. J. realize this himself. When he establishes himself as the club's leader, the players will follow him to glory." But Saban didn't stop there. O. J. had been with the Bills for three frustrating, heartbreaking years in which he ran against stone walls because he had no men to set him free. Then along came Reg McKenzie.

This fellow, just turned twenty-three, became the leader of the Simpson brigade. McKenzie spearheaded an offensive line that enabled the one-time USC star to gain over two thousand yards in 1973—a record which crushed Jim Brown's mark. Yet O. J. and McKenzie and his marauding blockers were only half of the story because you have to defend, too. It was as if the defense suddenly determined to outdo the offense, and at season's end there was no stronger team playing the game than the Buffalo Bills.

Two years after his return to Buffalo, Coach Saban had his club believing in itself, and, though the cliché reminds us that one rose doesn't make a summer, what happened in 1973 was the result of complete and thorough rebuilding. It was the establishing of solid and youthful foundations which now will be strengthened against the years to come—years that will bring what this Bills' unit needs for greatness: experience.

Owner Wilson has been castigated by many because of his determination to get a few things going his way. Regarded as a savior when he first hit our area, he was cast suddenly in the role of a miserly villain once the team jelled and a buck was to be made. No other individual of local stature gave Ralph Wilson the time of day in 1959 when he risked his financial future on the potential loyalty of this area's fans. People forget, it seems, but if it means anything at all to Ralph Wilson, I have not forgotten, along with many others, and will be eternally grateful to him for the unalterable fact that he alone came to Buffalo and restored us to major professional status.

The return of the Bills and the sense of pride all Buffalo and area fans feel in the club and in its future seems to ease much of the frustration that all hands suffered during the ruinous years from 1966 through 1972. What is particularly thrilling about this ultimate promise of a solid football tomorrow is the fact that so much team effort is reflected in its accomplishment.

Lou Saban would be the first man to decry any suggestion that he came by this miracle alone. If he created a rebuilding miracle, he realizes that all who were a part of the overall conquest played equal parts with him.

The Bills represent the complete team effort—from every conceivable standpoint. It's the name of the game—any game.

THE SABRES

During the years 1940–1941 professional hockey came to Buffalo in the spangles of an entry in the American Hockey League. There was no prediction that, as the years matured this organization, it would become as successful a venture as would ever make the grade in the sport outside of the National Hockey League. That was accepted as fact because this area is only a silver dollar's toss across the Niagara River to Canada, which germinated the hockey seed so many, many years ago. In the thirty-year lifetime of the Buffalo Bisons, they ruled the minor hockey-league kingdom year in and year out.

When early plans were formulated to create this fertile hockey area into major acreage, no thought was ever given to whether a Buffalo entry in the NHL would succeed or fail. It was simply a question of finding the right name, enlarging the Memorial Auditorium seating capacity to exceed fifteen thousand, buying off the AHL franchise, and setting up the organization. In those thirty so fruitful AHL years, Buffalo was still as close to the Canadian shore as always, hockey was still the dominant game in the Dominion, western New Yorkers were more demanding that they be represented in hockey's major circle, and you still couldn't buy, beg, or steal a seat for any game at Toronto's Maple Leaf Gardens. Through a contest, the fans selected the name Sabres. The Knox brothers, Seymour and Northrup—scions of one of the most dignified families of the nation—held the financial reins and purchased the rights to operate in the NHL from the Pastor brothers. These men had purchased the Bison franchise in the mid-fifties, and no part of the success of the Sabres could ever have been accomplished without the solid foundations which were further strengthened when the Pastors put all of their money, energy, and loyalty into their operation here.

The Knox brothers were joined by David Forman, a long-time associate, in establishing the front office. Forman is the operational head of the organization, and as with every other man who holds a key position in the Sabre scheme of things he is dedicated, demanding, and more knowledgeable with the passing of each season. The famed Punch Imlach was hired as general manager and coach of the club while Freddy Hunt, who had served the Bison club as general manager for eighteen years, became

54

Imlach's assistant. Since that beginning, the front office alignment has remained the same. In 1972, Imlach was forced to yield his coaching duties as the result of a severe heart attack. For a while it was feared that he would be forced out of the game entirely, but fortunately Punch played the game as the doctors prescribed, and today he is moving along in excellent shape.

Joe Crozier, long-time Imlach friend and associate, was brought in to take over the reins from the ill Imlach, and Crozier did an excellent job, which was never better illustrated than during the 1972–1973 season. After two years of expansion pains, and through the player manipulation genius of Imlach, the Sabres iced a team that third year that literally startled the hockey world. Two youngsters, Gil Perreault and Rick Martin, were culled from the Canadian amateur ranks and each became an instant star. Joined later by Rene Robert, this threesome, known as the French Connection and aided by the sensational goaltending of Roger Crozier and Dave Dryden, led the fledgling team to a position in the Stanley Cup play-offs. In losing to the ultimate winners, the Montreal Canadiens, in the first round, Buffalo threw a scare into the time-honored Canuck outfit that all but shook them into submission.

The fourth year, then, was to be the setting for a continuation of this incredible start for the Sabres, who play to a sellout every time they skate onto the ice. A third- or second-place finish in the eastern division was envisioned, for Imlach, never standing still, had created a tiger in the city of Cincinatti where Buffalo operates its AHL farm franchise. But it wasn't meant to be and that was true from before the actual 1973–1974 season began. You do not blame the failure of a team on injury alone; that is, you do not blame the entire failure of a team for that reason. In this instance—well, let me ask you to judge for yourself: Speedy wingman Larry Micky broke a leg before the season started. Perreault, a superstar in his second year, broke a leg just as the season began. Roger Crozier, top goalie for the Sabres, was hospitalized for recurring pancreatitis to the point where he was rendered almost completely inactive for the entire season. Red Schoenfeld, star rookie defenseman, was out early because of severe back trouble which resulted in exhaustive surgery. Then came the tragic death of the Sabres' "coach-on-the ice," Tim Horton. Tim died in a frightful automobile crash, and the club had lost its spearhead. Micky, as the campaign ran out of breath, broke his other leg. These injuries, mind you, were the ones that practically decimated the Sabres. Minor injuries were abundant—but so, too, were they plentiful for the other clubs in the league. At that, and despite it all, Buffalo didn't yield its play-off spot until the final week of the regular season.

So the Buffalo Sabres have grown to age four, and what next year and those which will follow will bring can only be guessed at. But we can be certain that, as an organization, Buffalo is as sound as any hockey team that plays anywhere in the world—that holding true for front office and player personnel—and western New York continues to take second place to none in the way its fans back their beloved heroes. The whole kit and kiboodle will be around a long, long time.

THE BRAVES

During the course of our meander with memory, the activities of the Bills—the old and new—and the Sabres have been pretty clearly defined, their structures explained, their plusses and minuses outlined. The Bills came first to give us major sports activity baptism—that has been established. Further, we have attempted to show how, once bitten by the major mosquito, we itched for a full-scale sports program in which was stressed only the top cut of quality sports meat with a farewell and thanks for services rendered to minor activity.

It was ten full years of major activity for the Bills before the Sabres were ready to replace the snorting Bisons of the American Hockey League. Once his head had been lopped off by a powerful swipe of the new sword, the Bison, who lost one life as a baseball symbol, lost the second of the only two he had as hockey traded major for minor. The Bison is possibly the fastest fading breed of animal anywhere in the world, but our own pet Buffalo Bison, who fought so gallantly and for so long and with such distinction, became extinct within a span of a single decade.

The third seeker of the major mantle in the area of western New York appeared as a basketball franchise in the National Basketball Association—The Buffalo Braves. A New York syndicate, headed by Carl Scheer, moved into Buffalo and started operations in 1970. The organization had been able, through the use of mirrors I have always thought, to lure Eddy Donovan away from the New York Knickerbockers of the same NBA. Any man conversant with the sport realizes that Donovan, as Knick boss under President Ned Irish, was as qualified as any man on earth to head up new proceedings in a new community. The question was a simple one: Just what tactic was required to pry him loose from his Knickerbocker locker room?

There were two solid reasons for Eddy to leave the scene of his greatest conquest and come to Buffalo. One, and possibly the strongest, was that his wife wanted to come back to the familiar terrain that she and Eddy called home—Olean, New York, the home of St. Bonaventure University, where Donovan came to his initial fame as coach of the Brown Indian basketeers. The second reason was that Donovan had climbed the mountain at New York, and the challenge, therefore, was simply to start again. There is a vast difference between this and the fight to achieve, and I do believe that the new quest, plus the chance to come home, proved too potent an opportunity to toss away. Also, Eddy would be given five percent of the franchise, along with a beautiful bouquet of bucks, and this had to carry a bit of weight, at least.

So Scheer had Donovan to run his club, and obviously he needed a man to coach. Dolph Schayes, one of the greatest players in the history of the NBA, was offered the job of directing the Braves on the court, and he accepted the job and a two-year contract to do just that. I took on the public relations task while Jerry Kiseel was hired to handle publicity. Jerry McCann, a master trainer and road secretary, signed on in that dual capacity, and one by one were players added to floor the first major pro team in an established professional basketball league in the history of the city of Buffalo.

When the 1972 season ushered in the Braves' third campaign, only Eddy Donovan, of the original cast, was still in the employ of the organization. Just as the first year started, a Buffalo millionaire by the name of Paul Snyder came in and bought the club, lock, stock, barrel, headaches, and everything else save for Donovan's five percent. Snyder's idea, a good one, was to make the entire deal local for local consumption, and this became obvious immediately when he filled the director's posts with men of area prominence.

Snyder made one initial and glaring error which he has since corrected, and just in time. Paul Snyder founded and brought to greatness an organization by the name of Freezer Queen Foods. His success was achieved because he first learned the business in its every facet and then was wise enough to surround himself with people who were masters of their craft. Snyder literally exploded to his financial security because he was smart enough to guide and patient enough to allow his team to form. But when he assumed command of the Braves, he astounded all who knew him by deserting the philosophy of team effort which had established him as a genius in the business world.

Paul Snyder tried to run his club as a fan. Though he had Donovan and Schayes under contract, Snyder insisted upon calling the plays and kept a miser's grip on his money. He knew nothing of the intricate methods of conducting business on the major sports level, and he deserted one of his own tenets by refusing to put implicit faith in the knowledgeable men who had been to the well before and who therefore could handle each of the tricky operations necessary in establishing unity in the Braves.

For three years, and each must have seemed a separate eternity for Snyder, this pulling in opposite directions stymied the initial progress of Buffalo's entry in the NBA. A fourth such year would have meant certain defeat, and it must have become apparent to the owner who can stomach almost everything else except defeat. He suddenly faced himself with the fact that he had the fans, despite the failure of the team to even play ball with any degree of respectability, and he had Eddy Donovan, the miracle worker for the Knicks.

Starting with the 1973–1974 campaign, it was Snyder working with Donovan. The latter was given a free hand and a checkbook which came in for a serious trouncing. Coach Jack Ramsay had been hired the year before, and this was a master stroke. This former Philadelphia mentor is equally allergic to defeat, along with Snyder and Donovan, but he knows as well as anyone that victory doesn't come by wishing and it doesn't come cheap. One by one, the rungs were placed in the ladder: Bob McAdoo, who may one day be the most prolific scorer in all NBA history; Randy Smith, who cannot fathom his potential because he is better each time out; Garfield Heard and Jim McMillian, Donovan selections who have blossomed under Ramsay, became additional rungs. When the college draft came along, Donovan and Ramsay grabbed Ernie DiGregorio so fast that the kid from Providence, R.I., never had a chance to even blink his eyes. Only Bob Kauffman, of the originals, was retained. He was what power and what strength the sad Braves had, but Kauffman came up lame early in this most recent campaign and he knew that, after one more year, there would be no tomorrow. That year was spent with Atlanta.

As the fourth year wore on, there were fewer Snyder tantrums and more cohesion, which the team needed to jell. At one stage of the proceedings, and just when a lift was badly needed, Donovan pulled one of his Willis Reed masterpieces—he made a deal with the Houston Rockets that brought Jack Marin and Matt Goukas to Buffalo in exchange for two players who didn't figure in the Braves' overall plan for victory. This trade unified the club and enabled it, as the growing thousands of fans went berserk, to make the play-offs when, just a year before, there was talk of complete collapse.

As with the Sabres the year before, the Braves were called upon to face one of the truly great teams in the NBA in the first round of the 1974 play-offs. Buffalo, which hadn't won a single regular season game from the Celtics until deep into the 1974 campaign, gave those proud New Englanders a nightmare that they will never forget, and, at that, yielded only under the greatest cloud and amid the most confounding confusion that basketball has ever witnessed. The Braves lost the first game in Boston and then roared back to even the series at home. Game three went to the Celtics on their court, game four to Buffalo on theirs. The fifth game, in which the Braves led right to, but not including, the final gun, allowed Boston to take a 3–2 lead. In the sixth game of the best four out of seven, the Braves trailed by four points in Buffalo with ten seconds to go. But two miscues and two Brave dunks enabled Ramsay's club to tie at 104. Then Boston threw the ball in play, Jo Jo White took a shot and, according to top referee Mindy Rudolph, was fouled by Bob McAdoo with a second left on the clock. When White stepped to the free-throw line, the clock showed no time remaining, and more than 18,000 fans, from management on down to sweeper, went berserk. White ended the Brave dream by netting his penalty shots, and Boston moved on to the next round and the title.

It was a sad and frustrating finish for the Braves, but it alerted the entire world of professional basketball to the fact that, as with the Bills and the Sabres, the city of Buffalo, proud and strong, now had another star in the firmament of professional athletics.

Owner Snyder, typical of the way he does business, wound up his fourth season with his fists hammering at the door of the referees. Then he vanished into the night, taking the 1973-4 season, his fourth year, with him but promising to return. Any area needs its fighters and defenders. Paul Snyder is needed in Buffalo.

10

Thoughts from The Western New York Catholic

THE YEAR 1966 SAW ME ACCEPT A POST with the weekly western New York Diocesan paper, as conductor of a column, "The Human Side." It is still very much my column today, and as long as my typewriter is staffed with a ribbon I hope that it will always be. The late Bishop of Buffalo, James A. McNulty, and Tom Bennett, editor of the *Magnificat,* were the men who asked me to become an associate. They understood that I was a Lutheran and that was one of their reasons for wanting me on their staff—the encumenical value of such an association we believe to be important. The *Magnificat,* now known as *The Western New York Catholic,* is sent to approximately 100,000 families in the eight counties every week—and a Lutheran goes with each copy. To say that I am proud of that association is to be understating one of my greatest prides. Somewhere Martin Luther is proud, too.

The following are a few columns that mean a lot to me.

LEADERS ARE BORN NOT MADE
It was during the middle of the Buffalo Bills' American Football League season in 1962 that the youngster traded uniforms. The deal that brought Jack Kemp from San Diego to Buffalo didn't shake the earth or any portion of football's sod.

Actually there was a touch of humor to it. The Bills, for a hundred bucks, had latched on to a quarterback with a broken middle finger on the right, or throwing hand. Of such trivia are trivial stories created only, at a seemingly justified appointed hour, to die aborning. This story didn't die because it was created by a man who was born to live and to lead.

The Kemp of those almost dozen years ago was no different, really, from the man I sat beside at the Cheektowaga Little League awards banquet in the Cordon Bleu just two weeks ago. Oh, yes, he had come to his football man's estate in the ensuing years using this stocks in trade—ability, courage, discipline and an almost incredible belief in himself—as a master painter culls from his own genius and interprets it on canvas. But back then, and as you watched him grow, you knew that no part of what could be honestly described told the basic story of the man. Meaning that no man can find just the right phrasing to explain the almost indefinable quality of leadership in another man. It lives in a man and it is felt by other men but it cannot be graded or weighed and no one can ever explain it.

Jack Kemp led the Bills to AFL supremacy in 1964 and again in 1965. He was the inspiration for that achievement by the teams as well as its on-the-field main architect for victory. Later a freak accident in pre-season training cut him out of action for a whole season and it was during that time that the maturing Kemp took stock of himself. For Jack his life was not to be an entire devotion to the sport of football. He had learned much from it and he owed much to it because of that chance to learn. But the time came to quit that which had given him so much. The time came for him to put into complete context the quality of leadership that had enabled him to emerge as one of the fine craftsmen of professional football. The time came for giant strides after a long succession of important little steps. The time came to prove, again, that leaders are born and not made.

As we sat with such as Bob Kauffman, Frank Swiatek, George Daddario and John Leypoldt the other night, Jack and I looked out at the throng of Cheektowaga family people who had come to savor the rewarding climax to the year's athletic achieving by both their girls and their boys. Kemp looked at the men and the women along the speaker's table. He looked at the young athletes and at their mothers and fathers, their sisters and their brothers. Then he said: "This is good, Ralph. This is where the greatest lessons are learned—this world of athletics. And these youngsters, looking from their seats up to these fine athletes sitting with you and me, are seeing themselves in their images. We are lucky because we have been given the privilege to set the examples. They are lucky," finished Jack Kemp, "because they know of the dedication of their coaches and their teammates and, even to a greater degree, they are learning the meaning of loyalty as it should be taught—by their own families through their own loyalty."

It was as Jack's voice became a kind of whisper mingling with the hum of general conversation that I saw, again, the look on his face when he first announced his intention to run for political office. It was the face of a leader ready to lead. Jack Kemp set his standards high from the very beginning. He became the Congressman from the 38th District in a landslide. He was honest enough to admit that his fame as a footballer aided tremendously. But the world was honest enough to admit that what he showed in leadership on the football field were the qualities which he needed to represent us in Washington. How right he has proved the world to be.

Ever since his first day as a Congressman Jack Kemp has walked forward with never a backward glance. He has demonstrated over and over again the basic honesty that is his birthright. He has bowed to no man and to no party and he has never forgotten a single mile of the many miles it took for his long walk from a busted finger to today when he is respected and revered for his leadership.

Through my interesting years, and without belaboring the point, I have contended that the lessons learned "on the fields of friendly strife" are as valuable and as enduring as any learned in any other fashion. Jack Kemp learned those lessons well as witness the fact that he stands today in total respect and with only his onward years to lead him to greater stature. May he embrace them in good health.

HE RAN AND HID IN HISTORY

It was Joe Louis, with the mightiest fists of all, who gave the classic answer when asked: "He says he will outbox you, Joe, and take your title on a decision." Joltin' Joe, as verbally retiring as any man who ever lived, didn't lack for the right words when he said: "He can run but he cannot hide."

For no particular reason this reflection of one of my alltime favorite people hit me right between my eyes as I watched Secretariat the other day at Woodbine which outskirts Toronto. It was the final appearance of the most tremendous thoroughbred since Citation and it was proper that this class animal should give his farewell performance against the class backdrop of Woodbine and the Ontario Jockey Club. Secretariat, that drippy Sunday afternoon, ran his adversaries into the sog and when he had established a commanding lead at the top of the stretch and looked to his green pastures just beyond the wire he let loose with a tremendous rush.

As he literally sailed to his blistering, annihilating victory in the Canadian International he ran and he ran and he ran and then, four hooves over the finish line, Secretariat hid—in the pages of history. There is room for him there as he joins the hallowed legion of great thoroughbreds who raced before him. As with his stablemate Hall of Famers Secretariat will never be forgotten. The racing world has known that since this dominant, red-hued mammoth won the Belmont to nail down the Triple Crown. But it became accepted fact that Sunday at Woodbine.

That rainy day people didn't go to the races, as such. And lots of people who were there for the final rung to be placed in Secretariat's ladder to horse immortality had never been there before. Such was the magic of the horse—such is the magic of the sports world. It was a day dedicated to a farewell tribute to a champion and it was as if you knew that Secretariat understood and was grateful for the tremendous outburst of affection.

It all began early and long before the eighth race which was the swan song special. People, many of them, wanted just one thing, really. To see Secretariat in the flesh and to be able to say to others in years to come: "Yes, I was there when he ran his last race." This must be truth for when I had muscled my way to the paddock, and been much muscled in return, and headed for a vantage point in the stands I actually saw people leaving for their cars BEFORE the race. They had seen Secretariat—he was what they had come to see.

Somehow I managed a three-by-three (inches) observation point. From there I watched the horses enter the track and from there I heard the imcomparable Darryl Wells introduce them by number and by name. When Kennedy Road was identified the throng gave this Canadian favorite a tremendous round of applause. But when Number 12 was presented it was the scream of Belmont Park relived. Such a tribute few athletes have ever been paid and, in my time, no other horse. The fact that the redoubtable Ron Turcotte was not atop Secretariat made no difference whatsoever. This was a horse's day—a very special horse.

After the start and after the first turn it was Kennedy Road in the lead and Secretariat at his tail. They sped along devouring turf with their hooves and the throng never eased its uproar. Then, as the turn was made off the back stretch and Secretariat moved in front, Woodbine erupted. As if accepting this as a final tribute to his greatness Big Red (ever reminding thoroughbred racing of another Big Red) went to his ultimate glory. Kennedy Road faded back into the field as the field faded back into a special rooting section of its own. Alone, with the wind and the rain in his mane, streaked the proud king of all racing.

Secretariat finished as if impatient to be done with the competition. He ran and he ran and he ran and why not? He had a date with destiny and the king wasn't to be denied. On October 28th, 1973, Secretariat ran and he hid and you'll not find him again unless you thumb the pages of history.

Yes, I was there when he ran his last race. And, yes, I have a little oblong piece of paper to prove it. For one infinitesimal period of time a horse managed to change my heartbeat to a hoofbeat. It was one of my greatest thrills during a lifetime of sports thrills. My thanks to the donor—SECRETARIAT.

MEMOIR OF A FRIEND

There were four of us sitting around the United Press news room on the 17th floor of the Rand Building. There was Maggie Wynn and there was her boss, Ed Feinen. The other two were interlopers from the office next door. One was WGR news chief Jack McLain and the other was a sportscaster who even then went by the name of Hubbell. The year was 1946 and the conversation was just as it is in most news rooms—chewing the fat. The clock suggested that time was awasting and, thus, further reminded us that we were paid to pound typewriters and woo microphones and not to chew the fat. And then the lad walked in.

The lad, he appeared to be about 13, asked for Mr. Feinen and, as if on signal, the radio rounders went back to their own diggins. About a half hour later our door opened and Feinen had his young man in tow. Eddie said: "Jack and Hub this is UPI's newest gift to the world of wire-service journalism. Meet Jack Horrigan." So we dutifully shook hands with Mr. Horrigan (I had a difficult time refraining from calling him Jackie) and wished him luck and health in his new career. Then, thinking that UPI was carrying this idea of starting them young a little too far, the door between the two offices closed and life, through newsgathering eyes, brains and fingers, went on.

As time led us away from that first meeting with Jack Horrigan we learned a great deal about the young man who wasn't 13. He was 21, with a solid war record as part of his credentials, and he had but one attitude: To keep looking, thinking and working forward in a dedicated desire to become the best newsman in the field. He excelled from the very start but Jack Horrigan, as versatile a man who ever blessed this world, had many goals and not just sights for one target. His basic love was people and his basic ingredient was decency and he simply took his life plan from that devotion to himself and to mankind. That such a philosophy should lead him into the field of public relations was only natural which explains why, four years after that day we all met for the first time, Horrigan became associated with the Buffalo Hockey Bison organization as its publicity chief. Jack spent four years with the ice machine before he accepted a writing post with the Buffalo Evening News. Five creditable award-winning years later he was named chief of publicity for the American Football League. Horrigan ended his wanderings when, in 1966, he took over as vice president in charge of public relations for the Buffalo Bills—a title he accepted but always regarded as cumbersome. Jack wasn't a title kind of guy.

The foregoing is the chronological order of events in the work-a-day life of Jack Horrigan who, after one of the most tenuous, frustrating yet courageous battles for survival in the history of mankind, died on June 2nd, 1973. Jack Horrigan moved on leaving a veritable legacy of love and, for those of us who knew him best because we worked closest to him, he will never be replaced nor will it ever be possible, in any measure whatsoever, to do full justice to his contribution to the community he adored and for which, and in which, he dedicated the too short years of his life.

For Jack Horrigan the seven year war is over. Who are we to judge his death or the manner in which it was accomplished? If all we do is cry and bemoan his departure then we do Jack Horrigan, and every wonderful thing he represented, a disservice which, at no time, did he ever merit. He taught us the meaning of friendship and humor and he, as much as anyone else, wrote the book on courage. When I think of him in every tomorrow there will be no tear in my eye but there will be a smile playing tricks with my lips. For he was that kind of person and you had better believe he was that kind of person for even when the going was the roughest and the pain was the harshest upon meeting you he would ask: "How are YOU feeling?"

For Jack the warring years are over and for his marvelous family his death must come as surcease and, as the pain eases, it must be replaced by a strong continued feeling of pride in the manner in which he lived and in the world's spontaneous spirit of tribute to him in his passing.

Gentleman Jack has gone home leaving us lonelier but infinitely better for his having touched us all.

I NEVER KNEW THEM

Although it is not ours to reason the time of our arrival upon this earth nor the time of our departure from it I believe that it is our privilege to question any series of circumstances which remove a stalwart individual from among us before his time. In dealing with this I refer, specifically, to a tall titan from the world of sports. In referring to his death "before his time" we assume that his death occurs before what we believe to be his normal life's span has been run.

Perhaps, in his wisdom, God gives to each of us an hourglass by which to measure the span of each of our lives. And when that glass has run shy of its sand He calls us home. These were my sobering thoughts when, such a few, short days ago, my car radio intoned the shocking news that Tim Horton, Buffalo Sabre defenseman, had died in a fearsome car crash on the Queen Elizabeth Way while returning to Buffalo from Toronto.

Inasmuch as I retired from in-the-field sports reporting before Tim Horton came upon the Sabre scene our paths, as individuals, never crossed. However, the fact that I did not know him personally in no way lessened the impact of his composite contribution to the world of hockey as a man of compassion, ability, dignity and class on me. By his very manner of conduct and by his strength which was demonstrated in so many ways in the heat of combat I knew Tim Horton to be a man of genuine class. So will he ever remain in memory. Men of sinew and fibre do not fade easily from the mind's eye.

As I drove along that sad morning, reflecting on the many aspects of such a tragedy, my thoughts went back over the years and my mind conjured up the faces of three other men—of the

Horton mold—who went to their Valhallas before, or so I believed, the sand had run shy of the glass. Three other men who I never knew as personal friends but men who became symbols of strength through their abilities on the fields of athletic contest and their compassion away from those fields.

The first of these was Lou Gehrig. This bemuscled, ice cold, brilliant and powerful first baseman of the New York Yankees literally was here one day and gone the next. Gehrig ran an unbelievable string of consecutive games in which he played—a record number which no one man will ever be allowed to approach for his own physical safety's sake—right into his grave. Gehrig knew that there was something drastically wrong when he went to his boss, Joe McCarthy, and said that he would have to end his string—the pain in his back was too great. There was a tear-streaking, mumbling farewell by Columbia Lou at home plate in Yankee Stadium—and in no time at all Gehrig the Great was dead—withered to dust. No, I never knew Lou, either.

Nile Kinnick, greatest quarterback and sports hero of his time, was the second man who came to memory's focus that morning, so few sad mornings ago. No college athlete ever captured the heart of America as did this bull's-eye Hawkeye Iowa thrower of 30 years ago. Kinnick never had even a remote chance to go on to greater heights in professional ball once he became a fighter pilot in World War Two. His death, of the four, is the most easily understood. He simply went out on a mission one day and Kinnick didn't come back. That happens in wars. You didn't have to know him personally to know what he was, either.

Roberto Clemente, strictly a product of today, charged my mind with his vigor, his tremendous ability, his love of all people. As with Kinnick, Clemente, too, went on a mission from which he failed to return. His was a mission of mercy and even today the stubborn waters which serve as his grave refuse, as they will for all time, to give back his body. Roberto Clemente's story was written to its conclusion when he became a member of baseball's Hall of Fame—the usual five year period of waiting waived in deference to his talent, his compassion and the reaction to his pathetic death. You knew Clemente personally just by realizing what he was, what he meant to his game and to his world.

And Tim Horton was number four.

Gehrig, Kinnick, Clemente and Horton—they played it full distance and fair. They made believers out of thousands of youngsters and they represented all that was good and consecrated the meaning of why we play our games. Only God knows why each was called home in this fashion. We say: "Before his time." We also say, to God on high, "Thy will be done."

REGGIE

When Reggie McKenzie came "bellering" into his world, 23 years ago, his Mom and his Pop were delighted, of course. But there was a certain sameness about the procedure which bordered on the old hat. It wasn't the prideful thrill of the first born McKenzie for the parental duo. As a matter of fact it was their sixth welcome party with two to come. McKenzies 7 and 8 arrived a year later, together, to complete a family that, through the years, was to grow strong as it grew together.

As I suggest it wasn't the thrill of the first born but it was as important as the first or the second or the third through to the eighth. For even a short while spent with this remarkable young man convinces you that his strength is born of the strength of the unity, decency and dedication of the entire McKenzie clan—the McKenzies of Detroit, Mich. Each boy McKenzie and each girl McKenzie is as important as the others and when you believe as I believe—that our basic strength as a nation depends upon the individual basic strength of each family that dwells therein—then you can know that Reggie's family has made its contribution and will continue to stay strong.

Twice, in recent weeks, I have had the opportunity to study, at close range, this broth of an individual who has just turned man from boy. The first time was when we sat together on the stage of the Auditorium in Attica. The second time was when he and I drove together to Jamestown to attend the 23rd annual Temple

Hesed Abraham father and son sports night. My deepest impression of him today is of a man, born to star in athletics, who realizes with deep conviction that he is also born to lead and, therefore, has an added duty to his fellow man to conduct himself with a quiet dignity that belies his years.

McKenzie is a big man as small skyscrapers go. He is called upon to speak and the audience response is instantaneous, lasting and impressive. He is given acclaim and reception that, as an athlete, he has not justly earned as yet. True, he came of age last year with the Bills as the lead blocker for O. J. Simpson. But a rose doesn't make a summer and a season of brilliance doesn't earn you your one way ticket to a cubicle in football's professional Hall of Fame. It's over the long haul that you prove your right to the stature of legend in athletics and, with a nod from Lady Luck and the full blessing of God, Reggie will find his stall waiting for him at his career's end. The stuff is there—but Father Time, who can outrace the wind, won't hustle for a soul if he feels he's being rushed.

What makes McKenzie that little bit different is his attitude and his compassion for others. Not only is he a winner—with his every motivation victory—but people, even at this early stage, realize it. Thus, when he suddenly appears before them, they see in him a quality that is a little something extra—and if it needs a name you can call it charisma, class, dedication, positive attitude—or pick one of your own—or combine 'em all. After he is introduced and the applause fades the silence which greets this tall young man is twice as deafening as the acclaim. When he breaks that silence it is in a low key voice that commands attention.

But it is what he says that counts because what he says makes sense. None of the corn that characterizes most of the banquet buddies. There is none of the boast about him. He is a believer in himself—not a trumpet for his accomplishments. Two minutes after he starts he stops. But you have received his message. That the tree grows tall if the soil is good is a fair way to describe what Reggie McKenzie imparts to the people who listen to him. As the years pass more and more people will listen to him.

71

If O. J. Simpson is the inspirational leader of the Buffalo Bills then take it from an old salt and believe that O. J. is led by a leader—Reggie McKenzie. Just 23 years ago this man came into the world. Just two years ago he came of competitive age. And he is going to take a whole football team and a half a million fans with him in his climb to the top. Take a lesson from the McKenzie book—learn strength from your family, take strength from your family so that you may give strength to your nation.

At visit's end today may I pause just this briefly to thank you for your tremendous loyalty to me and to my family over the runaway years. On February 10, I marked my 39th anniversary as a reporter of sports in Buffalo, Western New York and Ontario. No part of any of that journey would have been possible without Ann and, as the years outraced themselves, Peter, Phil, Emmy and a succession of dogs.

Of my walk through the years may I say that it has been a lovely walk in which I enjoyed living in each today, in which I sought to remember the best of all of my yesterdays and eagerly and always anticipated the promise of my tomorrows.

And, by golly, the journey's just begun.

Congressional Record

United States of America

PROCEEDINGS AND DEBATES OF THE 93^d CONGRESS, FIRST SESSION

Vol. 119   WASHINGTON, FRIDAY, JUNE 15, 1973   No. 93

House of Representatives

RALPH HUBBELL SPEAKS FOR AMERICA

Hon. Jack F. Kemp of New York in the House of Representatives, Friday, June 15, 1973.

Mr. Kemp, Mr. Speaker, outstanding prose, that which contains eloquence as well as substance in the same essay, is a rare discovery. When it does appear, therefore, it should be shared.

Such prose flowed from the pen of my friend, Ralph Hubbell recently in his own column, "The Human Side," which appears in Buffalo's Magnificat Catholic Weekly. The Hubbell essay is a personal interpretation of "America, the Beautiful."

Its style, grace, and elegance make it compelling.

The essay follows:

WATERGATE
By Ralph Hubbell

O BEAUTIFUL FOR SPACIOUS SKIES

Clear, blue skies to beckon our eyes and beseech us to look up with pride in this land of ours and beyond, with reverance and hope, to God Almighty who forgives us our troubled times in the knowledge that our ship is a proud ship and that our way is a proud and progressive way—and is not a lost way.

FOR AMBER WAVES OF GRAIN

Showing the whole wide world of people how bountiful are our resources and how distant are our horizons. Farmlands that nourish and strengthen us and remind us of our God-given heritage and of our freedom which may be challenged but which, until the end of time, will rally from any attempt, from within or without, to bind our hands, seal our lips, blind our eyes or impair our progress.

FOR PURPLE MOUNTAIN MAJESTIES

Mountains, they mean, for us to look up to and beyond, again, to the highest reaches where God lives and where God loves us all. Mountains, they mean, not for us to stand upon as busy-bodies seeking to solve the problems of the world and not as would-be conquerors of that world but as fortunate people seeing from on high the beauty of the world and willing to share our own bountiful treasures of peace and freedom with that world.

73

ABOVE THE FRUITED PLAIN

Upon which plain we all stand shaken today in the knowledge that our chief causes for concern and unrest have festered from within. Yet upon which plain we promise as one that we will stay united as we seek our solutions with strong faces looking confidently to one another. We promise, as one, a unison of purpose and a self-belief that once our record has been cleaned of all taint and once we have put our own house in order in our own way we can walk, with pride, in the sun again.

AMERICA, AMERICA GOD SHED HIS GRACE ON THEE

Yes, indeed, He shed His grace and His compassion upon all of us the while He knows that no matter how muddled the waters they will clear with hope and self-dedication to purpose: He knows that no matter how high the hurdle we will conquer it as we clear the air; He knows of troubles past and He watched, and was proud, when we set our house in order and continued the joyous road that is our beloved America.

AND CROWN THY GOOD WITH BROTHERHOOD

That has been our key for our salvation from the very first step that was taken upon our soil by the very first people who yearned to be free and to stay free. Brotherhood is just that. It is the acceptance of each other as a brother but not just within the circle of our own family. Brotherhood goes beyond our shores and insists that we accept all people as brothers for all people, one day, must be free. It is as brothers that we can re-unite to find our way back to the dignity and decency which we knew and accepted, perhaps too lightly, before the black cloud of doubt hovered over us and saddened us—so.

FROM SEA TO SHINING SEA

It is as a shining family that we will one day continue as a self-believing family once the wisdom for realizing our shortcomings and for ferreting out and punishing our traitors is blended with

74

the further knowledge that something must be done swiftly and with lasting strength and decisiveness. From the Atlantic to the Pacific we are America. Between those shores a pitiful and faithless few have been allowed to undermine, in some measure, all that we hold dear and all that we feel is our pride and our possession. It is when our freedom is challenged—from within as well as without—that we prove ourselves America at our integral best. Conquer we must and we will and let us lift our hearts to God in the certain belief that America is today, and will ever be, America, the beautiful.

11

A Word About Children

THE ISN'T ANY WAY OF KNOWING just when I became convinced that the most important individual in the world is a child. Perhaps it was the dedication of Tem that planted the seed, because if a person that complete, that meaningful, that deeply intelligent, could sacrifice her entire future for children then she must have believed the same thing. The child is the world's tomorrow, and therefore only a strong tomorrow could be fashioned with strong boys and strong girls. It wasn't just because Albert, Phil, and I were Tem's sister's children that she gave us so much of her life. That was the original motivation, of course, but she must have come to realize that just caring for us, just seeing to our needs, wasn't enough. We needed love and discipline, and we needed teaching.

My interest in youngsters began almost as a necessity for, at Westminster House in 1931 and at Little Italy for the next two years, that's all we dealt with. Kids, as with warts, simply grow on you, and as Ann has said so many times (but never in any critical way) I am simply a sucker for a youngster and my only wish is that I will always feel this way.

Many years ago I wrote a poem which pretty well sums up the way I feel about the wee ones. As you read it, just roll with the lines and maybe the next time your world gets out of sorts and frustration is eating at you, instead of going for an aspirin or a beer or a walk, reach out and take hold of the hand of a little boy or little girl. Then walk and talk, and above all listen.

When your world is weary and you hit a snag
And your out of gas like a cornered stag,
When a heap o' livin' is a hollow alloy
Go live in the world of a little boy.

Go find what he finds in a full day's span
When he's dreaming his dreams and becoming a man.
Just sit on the sidelines and watch him grow—
You were a little boy once, you know.

The trouble with me and the trouble with you
Is just that we THINK we have too much to do.
We bend 'neath the weight of our daily strife
And forget there's joy and fun in life.

But the little boy doesn't—ah, no indeed,
To trouble and worry he pays slight heed,
He merely goes forward in spite of the world
And leads the parade with banner unfurled.

A friend of mine said to me one day
After he'd heard what I had to say:
"Your theory is fine for the few—not the crowds—
A world can't progress with it's head in the clouds."

Can't it—must we always have feet to the sod?
With your head in the clouds you're closer to God.
When your world goes wrong and it will you know
And you seek the lost beauty of sunset glow
Hitch your troubles to a small tot's toy
Go live in the world of a little boy.

78

The only explainable reason why those thoughts relative to a small boy came to me more than thirty years ago was obviously in the fact that most of my actual dealings were with them and not with little girls. But my priceless collection of children in the years since then has been gathered equally, and I definitely subscribe to what Frank Shorter, who won the marathon at the 1972 Olympics in Munich for his Uncle Sam, had to say to a reporter when asked this question, "As you ran your twenty-six miles plus were you conscious of the people along the way?" Shorter smiled and said, "I heard the laughter of little American girls. No one in the world laughs quite like a little American girl."

As I mulled over the challenge of writing this book I gave a lot of thought to the simple little visits which I had had with the children over the years. And I concluded that if succeeding generations of children enjoyed those visits, and could learn something from the messages which were plainly written therein, then most certainly I would include them in this segment of our overall walk together. Perhaps, in reading it, you will find much of your children there and, which is entirely possible, much of yourself there as well. You would do me a favor if you would read it aloud to your youngsters some early September and just before school starts. If it is, as the song suggests, a long, long, way from May to December then, for those who are coming off a summer in the sun, it's a fur piece longer from September to June again. This may make it a shorter, a more productive, a more meaningful distance for them to travel.

So tomorrow you go back to school. So tomorrow you start doing what we all have been doing since last you looked at a school book in June, working. Then, son and sister, join the club again.

A long while ago, maybe when your Mom and Dad were sitting in those seats and getting ready to go back to school themselves, I suggested that a little time spent together on this night might be for them, as well as for me, a worthwhile visit. Now that you have come along, and they realize the importance of what we talk about on this night, you might enjoy the same visit, the same chat together. One day, in reading something, somewhere, I chanced upon this suggestion: "That which is used develops; that which is not used wastes away." Tonight, as we sit quietly together, that is meant to apply to you as well as to me. THAT WHICH IS USED DEVELOPS; THAT WHICH IS NOT USED WASTES AWAY.

It means, very simply, that it is up to you what happens to you. Whether you are just beginning, with the fresh and saucy look of kindergarten; whether you are beginning to move into second gear in 4th grade; whether you are impressed with grammer school farewell; whether you are first year and fresh as fruit in high school; whether you are sassy and sophmore; whether you are safe and senior; whether you are college and, seemingly beyond knowledge, makes no difference at all. Each of you, in whatever category claims you, has God given talents which are yours to either develop and use to the fullest or, without accepting the challenge, allow to rust and waste away. If going back to school leaves a little, or maybe a lot, to be desired it is with the idea of trying to fit school into the idea and scheme of everyday living again that we take this time out. Meaning that no one expects any youngster, of any age, to believe that a hot dog or a swim can be equalled by geography or gym. The point is that all of us, and I mean ALL of us, have to accept the melancholy of mathematics as we accept the spiciness of a cookout—in stride.

Some years ago, after one of our chats, a youngster wrote to me and asked: "Did you ever go to school? You make it sound so nice?" Yes, I went to school, who doesn't? I further admitted that the day vacation ended, I wasn't thrilled by the thought of going back to school. But I also agreed that once the idea of vacation was over, once I knew how foolish it was to be afraid, once the feeling of doing something other than playing, once the rejoining of old friends made me enjoy old friends again, it wasn't so doggoned bad at all. We go to school to learn. Not just book knowledge learning. To learn how to live with and for other people. People, who, we may live with for years to come. Our own children made wonderful friends who are even better friends today and it is as a friend, and only a friend, that I visit with you tonight.

Here is all that I ask—that you give your teachers every possible chance to help you. As you look to tomorrow renew your faith in your parents, always your greatest friends, and your teachers, almost as close, who sometimes appear as ogres and tyrants only because of your own shortcomings. Give them a second thought, or a third if you can spare it, the while you remember that they are passing on to you what they spent countless hours and years, not to mention money, learning themselves. Think, seriously, of the priceless gift that is education. It's the synonym for progress—your own progress. Education is the only universal key that opens all doors to the future.

Years ago, when I started in radio, a college education wasn't too important. I was given a job because I had a working knowledge of the English language and a fairly listenable voice. It was all you needed then but it isn't all you need today. Today radio and television are fundamental parts of every college curriculum which means that every job that becomes available in this field is automatically highly competitive. But you can compete, in this field or in any other, if you are basically ready to compete.

Schooling is a part of your growing up. A part of the rich heritage that belongs to you in this place we call the United States. Thus if you waste any part of your education you are foolish indeed. Work hard, and concentrate as best you know, during the hours that school claims you. Then, after the bell rings, get out and play just as hard. The most wonderful thing about all living is that you can have everything you want, you can attain any goal, if you are willing to put everything you have into your effort. A school is your friend. Your teacher is your friend as are your Mom and your Pop. Use them as a mechanic uses his tools. Count them as blessings while they are yours to count. Look on everyone who is a part of your life as wanting to help you move forward and, as time goes by, you will find out that there is only one way to move and that is forward. ·

May I say again, and I have had occasion to say it so many,

81

many times, that I wish you well young friends. As you prepare to start school, continue it or finish it, grab your opportunities by the hand and when you are done with books and things be able to say because you have been honest with yourself: "This was my best." In looking at yourself remember that that which is used develops; that which is not used wastes away.

Good luck to you, wherever you are, from a person who thinks so very much of all of you and who knows, better than you can ever imagine, that you are tomorrow's adult and proud and intelligent America.

classic photo: Joe McCarthy and Lou Gehrig flank Babe
uth in St. Pete on a sunny day, in the long ago.

The most devastating power hitter in Buffalo International League history was Ollie Carnegie. Slow afoot—the restricted left-field acreage in Offerman Stadium allowed for this defensive deficiency—Carnegie had no peer in hitting for distance or cracking walls.

Jim Thorpe, one of the outstanding athletes of all time, is interviewed by a much younger Ralph Hubbell in Buffalo's Memorial Auditorium during a wrestling interlude thirty-three years ago.

be McCarthy, who will
e 88 on April 21, 1975,
njoys a bat of memory
vith the author.
McCarthy's animation,
is crystal clear memory
nd a willingness to share
is great life make him
ne of the truly great
nonuments to baseball.

O. J. Simpson on the play that set a new all-time record for yardage gained in one season—2003—against the New York Jets, December 16, 1973.

A jubilant O. J. being carried off the field at Shea Stadium by his joyous teammates.

Lou Saban, the man who has already given the Buffalo Bills two American League championships, is again leading the club back to the sun.

PHOTO BY ROBERT L. SMITH

The author in a characteristic pose—mouth open.

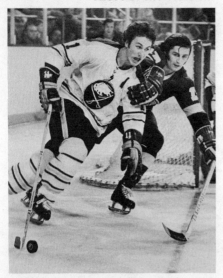

Gil Perreault—one of the National Hockey League's brightest young stars.

Rick Martin after scoring his fiftieth goal at end of 1973-74 season.

The late Tim Horton (#2) standing in front of his goalie, Roger Crozier.

No man ever had a greater impact upon one segment of athletic endeavor in a community than did Freddy Hunt on hockey in western New York. He is credited with being the most important individual in the transition of hockey in this area from minor to major.

Jim Schoenfeld wipes away tears as the Sabres observe a moment of silence before the game following teammate Tim Horton's death in an automobile accident.

Buffalo Braves' brightest star Bob McAdoo goes up against Kareem Abdul-Jabbar.

PHOTO BY ROBERT L. SMITH

Buffalo War Memorial Auditorium during a Braves game—it is considered one of the most beautiful and best sports arenas anywhere in the country.

12

One Man's Hall of Fame

JACK KEMP
WE DON'T HAVE TO BE CONSTANTLY RE-
minded of the basic soundness of the world of athletics by re-
peating a never-ending list of examples. The very nature of the
idea of playing games suggests important lessons for those who
play as taught by those who played before them and who, therefore, learned in the same manner. However, every so often a man
or a woman comes along who has learned the value of team
participation to the point of developing a selflessness that points up
the necessity for athletics. And one such individual was Jack
Kemp.

This athlete was the man who quarterbacked the Buffalo Bills
to their greatest victories when they dominated play in the American Football League. That was the league that merged with the
NFL to make pro football in the United States a one-world affair,
and Kemp was the fellow to whom everyone on those Bills teams
looked for leadership. This man, today a United States Congressman from the western New York area, played strictly for the team
and regarded his position on that club as something that had been
entrusted to him to develop and pass to others—and not just to his
teammates. The story of Kemp which I most like to tell—because I

believe it is so indicative of him, and also because it shows the true worth of the lessons learned in sports combat—concerns a day, just a scant few years ago, when the father of a very sick little boy called me on the phone.

This man's youngster was twelve years old, and before being bedeviled by leukemia was an active, football-saturated young man who, as with all kids everywhere, had his own pet idol. "My lad," said the father, "is in Sister's Hospital, and we have been alerted to the fact that if he makes it through another month he won't make it much beyond that." The pause was understandable. "Outside of the family, David looks to only one hero and that man is Jack Kemp." Again he paused before continuing. "I don't know how a person goes about such a thing, but I thought maybe you might be able to contact Jack, tell him David's story, and perhaps Kemp would be willing to stop in and just give him a smile or something."

When you deal with the class guy in athletics and you tell him a story of this nature, he doesn't just hear you out and pause before he says he will help. Kemp's very first reaction was, "How can I help? Tell me what I can do." Jack and I met at the hospital the next afternoon after I had found out the details concerning the room number, the right time, and so on. As we walked into the building, a silent Kemp was toting pictures, a football, and his own number on his own jersey. We walked straight to the lad's room, and found a nurse standing outside the door. She smiled at Jack and said, "David is waiting for you." Only David was waiting and only Jack went into his room.

As I lingered, and I wasn't in the mood for talking with anyone, I stared out the window. As I looked out on that very somber day, I recall thinking about some of the unfairness of the world. Why shouldn't a fine youngster such as David be given his full chance at life along with so many of the others who also played football and went to school and laughed? But when I start thinking that way I realize that I am over my head and that there is a pattern to life, or there are many patterns, and that someone, far wiser than I, establishes those patterns and does the planning.

After a little while the door opened, and Jack walked into the corridor and quietly closed the door behind him. Together we walked back down the corridor, and without a word Kemp got into his car and I drove home in mine. No, I didn't see David. David saw Jack Kemp, the man he had asked to see, and Jack saw David and left something, more than material, in his room.

CLINT BUEHLMAN

The year 1931, which was my record needle scratching beginning, also spawned the career of a man who must be regarded as the greatest single contributor to one radio area in the entire history of the profession. No story of my time or my world could ever be complete if it did not include more than passing reference to a man by the name of Clint Buehlman. This man, whose philosophy has always been to sell service rather than records or humor or gimmicks, began his announcing career in 1931 at WGR in Buffalo. The following year, Buehlman, whose idea of planting his roots deep in the soil of western New York was the same as mine, created what he called the "Musical Clock"—a time service, weather service, and news service program that started at 6 A.M. and continued through 9 A.M. Today, the same man with the same ideas has expanded his morning time period to ten o'clock.

Twelve years later, in 1943, Clint shifted his program to WBEN. He did so on his own terms, because his was the only program that WBEN couldn't beat in the ratings, and Buehlman has ruled the roost with an authoritative voice ever since. Today he is stronger than at any time in the past despite the never-ending effort put forth by other stations to unseat him from his throne as king of the area castle. It is entirely possible that Buehlman, whose programs have run every single day for forty years, may hold the record for longevity for any man associated with one program in the world of radio. When a station of the stature of WBEN admits

85

that it can't figure any way to beat you competitively and therefore has to buy you, you know that what you have to offer is solid gold and one product in a million.

Clint Buehlman's product is, of course, himself. Few men start from the blocks knowing just what their goal is. Clint will tell you that the most important radio time of the day is during the early morning hours from six to nine or ten. "That's when people plan their days," he says. "After ten o'clock they know just what their schedule will be, and therefore they don't have to know the specific time of day. But in the morning, as the plan is unfolding, that clock is their master. That's why I give the time every five minutes."

A close friend during the early years was a super salesman and a fine guy by the name of Nat Cohen. While Nat was in Chicago one day, he heard a morning man following the format that was one day to make Clint Buehlman one of the best-paid announcers in all radio. When Cohen returned to town, he took Clint aside and told him that he had found the vehicle that was best suited to Buehlman's talents. Clint heard Nat out and immediately balked at the idea. What kind of future, thought Clint, was in store for a guy who sat in front of a mike every morning and told people what time it was? Then, because his brain never misses a beat, he saw the wisdom of appealing to the early risers with a program they would listen to in a car as well as in their homes. So young Buehlman created his "Musical Clock," and in the forty years since he has never gone on the air without a sponsor. Today, with a four-hour stint Monday through Saturday, Clint broadcasts sixteen quarter-hour segments a day, each sponsored, and at the talent fee he commands, you don't wonder that the Buehlmans have three homes.

The Buehlman story is one that should be told to every person who contemplates *any* type of career—not just one in radio broadcasting. Clint's success spells out the value of being prepared with full knowledge of what you want to do and then working overtime to polish your talents. "When I was eight," Clint will tell you, "I was in a little radio play. And when I was eight, radio wasn't much older. But the bug bit me then, and later my mother insisted that I take a course in public speaking. It was laughable to me because that wasn't much of an art in those days, either." Then Buehlman paused before saying, "My mother was a most remarkably perceptive individual right up until her death at age eighty-five. So when she said that a public-speaking course would help me if I wanted to go into radio, that was what I would take. And I did and I am glad."

The area of western New York is generally believed to have three of the most celebrated attractions in the world. One is Niagara Falls, where lovers go. The second is Fort Niagara, where the historians go. And the third is Clint Buehlman, where listeners go.

FREDDY HUTCHINSON

Freddy Hutchinson was one of the first baseball men I covered, and for a single year he may have been as great as any in the game. Surely he was greater than most.

Hutch was born to pitch, and unless you were born to hit, he wasn't one of your favorites if hitting against him happened to be your livelihood. Though he was a nice guy when he was sitting in your living room, Freddy Hutchinson was all of the villains of the world rolled into one on the days he was going to pitch. Mind you, and mind well, he was nobody to be around from the time he awakened until long after his day's stint had been completed.

As the 1940s began, Buffalo had a working agreement with the Detroit Tigers. Our skipper then was Steve O'Neill, and Steve, who had been an outstanding catcher during his distinguished major-league career, carried much of his ability, and all of his compassion, on into managing ranks. He was overjoyed when the Tigers decided to send Hutchinson to him for a year of learning and work. Freddy was one of the first of the true bonus babies, and the Tigers wanted to make certain that when they sent him to the major wars he would be ready. Strangely, as you will understand

87

after I recite his amazing record of achievement while he was here for just one season, Hutch never made it as a pitcher in the American League. No one could quite understand it. And what made it all such a far greater mystery was that when he laid down his glove and went to managing, Freddy proved an instant success. How far he might have gone as a manager was never determined. After a brilliant start, Freddy Hutchinson's career and his life were simultaneously erased by cancer. The game and the world lost a big guy when Hutch went down.

Long before that, this man showed the world his talent and his temperament. He was long on talent, both as a pitcher and hitter, but he had one of the shortest competitive fuses of any man who ever played any game anywhere—and of most warriors famed in history. He just could not stomach the thought of losing, and therefore any man who played in a uniform other than the one he was wearing was considered a mortal enemy and was to be dealt with in the quickest and most decisive manner possible.

Hutchinson was constructed along the lines of a middle line backer. He was about six feet one and his muscles rippled through his uniform. He was built absolutely square, and his most aggressive and arresting physical feature was his chin. To say that he had a chisel chin would be to remember it with disrespect, for it was worth more than that expression conjures up. Actually it was a jutted jaw that seemed to carry it's own message: "So what are your plans, Mac?"

On the day of a game Hutch would arrive early, find himself his own little nook in the dressing room, and sit there until it was time to go through the preliminary motions of dressing and warming up. No one, not even O'Neill, ever said a single word to him at any time before his assignment. Once upon a time, I guess, someone must have done so and also must have paid an awful price. That story was never told, but, somewhere, there had to be a reason for such respect of another man's feelings. His actions on one of his pitching days were so unlike him, so paradoxical. He was a fun-loving guy, and he liked nothing better than a practical joke played on someone else, although he wasn't a spoil sport when someone played such an antic on him—as I recall few did. On days other than his work days he'd sit at the edge of the dugout, look up at our broadcasting perch, and have himself a fun time jawing with the crowd or baiting the umpire. Sometimes I wondered if he really enjoyed the game itself. There had to be some reason why Freddy Hutchinson was so great here and failed so utterly under the big top of the American League. The International then was better than what passes for major-league baseball today and Hutch dominated that league with such authority that he couldn't have failed in the majors because of any actual baseball deficiency. Dwelling on it is not going to solve what must be, to most, a long-forgotten problem, I realize. But thirty years ago, had you seen Freddy as we saw him, you would have concluded, as did we, that he was Johnson and Grove, that he was Mathewson and Earnshaw, and that stardom in the majors was his, just for the stroll to the mound. He simply never pulled it off.

Fred Hutchinson was a right-handed pitcher and a left-handed batter. So powerful was he at the plate that he was the first pinch hitter O'Neill called upon and it didn't matter whether the pitcher was throwing right or left. During the one year that Hutch played for Buffalo, he batted .393 and he missed winning the league batting crown—as a pitcher, mind you—by something like twenty-four times at bat. But great as he was with his menacing club—doubles were his specialty—he was the complete man, the superb man, from 60 feet, 6 inches out. He had speed pitches which appeared to increase in velocity as the game progressed. His curve was a fine pitch, but his change of pace was a virtual thief. It stole the eyesight right out of the batter's eyes and that man's bat motion was almost pathetic as he sought to put wood against the ball. Lest you gain the impression that I am creating a Bunyanesque character out of a blood and sinew being, let me assure you that this man was very, very real—he won twenty-nine games that year and lost only six. He started against Montreal ten times, he finished ten times, and he beat Montreal ten times. Three of his ten

89

conquests came in the play-offs, when Buffalo was eliminated, 4 games to 3, and I am certain that Hutch—who begged Steve O'Neill to pitch that seventh game with no day of rest and was denied the chance—never forgave his boss. Hutch had a way of remembering and smoldering as he remembered.

The unluckiest batter of them all was the lad who managed to clip Hutchinson for a home run early in the game. That unfortunate soul spent the rest of that game and the rest of that season, whenever Hutch was out there, scrambling for his life and dusting off his drawers. You simply did not insult Freddy to the point of walloping him for a homer and then expect him to say, "Nice goin', you hit one of my best pitches, Mac."

Yes, it is fact and fruitful memory that Freddy Hutchinson came upon our scene during the 1940–1941 season, that he put more into one campaign than most ball players put into five, that he went from here to Detroit with star written all over himself, that he was as bad there as he was good here, that he became a manager with tremendous potential, and that, as fate has a habit of doing once in awhile, he was felled by cancer and died in agony.

Of such men are memories made; of such men have books been written.

JOHN KONSEK III

John Konsek is a Buffalonian, and it was in western New York that he came to his greatest fame although two of his most treasured victories were established when he was an undergraduate at Purdue University. John Konsek played the greatest round of competitive golf that I ever saw, and as his story unfolds between these book covers and between these lines you may come close to agreeing with me.

Johnny Konsek was a strippling, in every sense of the word, when he dared upon the amateur golfing scene midway through my WBEN years. As with most youngsters with stars in their eyes, John entered every boys' and juniors' tournament he could find, winning many, losing some, seasoning well. His father, a hard-working individual, owned and operated a driving range, but he wasn't one of those over-doting fathers who couldn't see anyone else but his own son. He schooled his boy. He supported and was proud of John's activities, but he didn't commit the cardinal sin of over-zealous father and insist that the lad could do no wrong. The young man was disciplined, and he was taught the etiquette of golf just as diligently as he was taught the fine, basic points of playing the game. Along the way the son was taught the etiquette of life, too. When John Konsek was ready for the competitive wars, it was then that he was sent to the post and not a second before.

There was very little that Konsek didn't win, and he won everything of importance in the western New York area including the Porter Cup, an event sponsored by the Niagara Falls Country Club and fathered by Dick Harvey which is today rated as one of the three foremost amateur tourneys in the land. As an undergraduate at Purdue and as a member of the Boilermaker golf team, Johnny won two out of three Big Ten matches he played against Jack Nicklaus, who was solid gold even then.

As Konsek played, he never stopped improving because he never stopped trying to improve. When his brilliant career as a collegian was completed, the talk turned, quite naturally, to what this young man would do once he turned professional. There was much conversation and as much speculation because this lad was a better golfer every year. But those who were predicting his greatness as a pro were whistling in the dark because Johnny wasn't having any part of pro golf for even a wee portion of his future. Konsek wanted to become a doctor and John Konsek is today Dr. John Konsek—and you had better believe that he will be as good a doctor as doctors can be when the totals are added.

One year the Ryder Cup challenge matches were played at the Wanakah Country Club course near Lake Erie on the road to Cleveland. The American pros came to fight for position on the team that, every two years, vies with British shotmakers in an age-old competition. That year Chuck Healy and I televised the two-day affair—or what we could televise in the worst downpour in my memory—and among those competing was Dutch Harrison, the Arkansas Traveller, as likeable as he was big, rawboned, and able. One of the queries I put to Dutch was, "Do you fellows keep book on amateurs in the various areas around the nation?" Harrison, who smiled as slowly as he drawled, said, "We know the potential of every amateur, and it is important that we do. The young golfers are the ones who come to challenge us, and we find it important to know their abilities and thus the strength of their challenge to us." So I asked, "In this area, Dutch, what about the challenging young men?" Very frankly, because frankness was one of his stocks-in-trade, Harrison said, "There are only two boys here, and we don't worry about either one. You have a lad who hits long irons with the best on our circuit, but he can't putt. So he practices long irons. In this game, or any game, you practice your weaknesses, not your strengths." Dutch paused for a moment. "You have a second lad here, young Konsek, who has been discussed by our guys many times. However, we don't worry about him either. He has everything he needs to become a great pro, except one thing: He doesn't want to become a pro. He wants to become a doctor."

His greatest round of golf, which was the greatest I have ever seen, amateur or pro, was fashioned against the backdrop of the beautiful Park Country Club course in Williamsville. Williamsville, a suburb of Buffalo, had several courses to recommend it and which rate with the most pulchritudinous anywhere. Park Club is a fine, fearsome course when it is teed up for the long tourney hitters. That year Konsek was competing in the qualifier for the Buffalo District Golf Association title, and the best of our lot, and they were plenty good enough, were on hand to scrap it out. The course was dressed in its monster's robes.

The first two holes are par fives, and to assure you that I am not going over that round shot-by-shot I'll brief it up by saying that after those two holes Johnny was four under par. He turned the first nine in twenty-eight and he came home in thirty-three for a total of sixty-one, eleven shots under par. How do you do at your club?

That this youngster was set apart was obvious from the first time his inquisitive spectacles looked at me and his slightly shy voice said, ''I am happy to know you.'' He never lost his shyness, and I do believe, in a way, it proved to be one of his secret weapons. An opponent would take a look at Konsek, who for all the world resembled a flyrod with ears, and would literally feel sorry for him. Chuck and I remember Johnny for many reasons and not the least of these was his deep appreciation for those whom he believed were instrumental in shaping his career. Never able to rub more than a couple of dimes together at the same time during his learning years, Konsek always managed to send us each three golf balls with his greeting at Christmas time. Is it any wonder that I ask you to come walk with me and meet some of the treasured architects of my life?

BEN HOGAN

You didn't know John Konsek before this reading unless you are native to our heath or recall his feats in the Big Ten. But Ben Hogan, who used all of the grass, water, and sand of the courses of the world for his stage, is familiar to all of you although I have a hunch that when we move along you will know Ben Hogan better, you will admire him more, and you will respect him for the big man he became out of a small little world that once upon a time Hogan thought was his and his alone.

By some twist of events along the golfing tour and some fifteen years before John Konsek had made it to the first grade, the annual Western Open Golf Championships were played on another Williamsville course in our area. It was the Brookfield Country Club layout, and when dressed for the important visitors it was a fearsome animal that impatiently lay in wait for its celebrated guests. Normally, the event is played, as the name suggests, in the western part of the nation; memory fails to conjure up the why of it, but Brookfield hosted it that year and thousands of fans witnessed it. All of the titans of the late forties were present when tee-off time called the men to Thursday's start of play,

93

including Ben Hogan. They always referred to Ben as "Little Ben" or "the diminutive Hogan." Actually, though about 5'9" and 160 pounds top weight, he appeared to be small. He appeared to be small which he wasn't, and he appeared to be strictly for Hogan at all costs, which he was.

On the first day of the tourney, a young, tall, extremely good-looking and brilliant Buffalo golfer by the name of Mike Parco led the pack of world-famous shotmakers. Mike, still active in the pro teaching ranks here in the area, was so much at the top of his game back then that he managed to come home in front after thirty-six holes as well. Although Parco wasn't aware of it at the time, blind in his ecstacy, he had sealed his own doom. The touring pros enjoy their own little closed corporation, which does not at any time include an upstart professional who is strictly a local hero. So they try everything, short of kidnapping, to eliminate the budding star who they consider to be a thief in the night and after what rightfully belongs to them.

On the third day, Mike was sent off the tee with Jimmy Demaret, one of golf's great guys, and Hogan, the villain of our piece. Not once during the entire eighteen-hole route did Hogan look or speak to Parco. While this psychological harpoon was digging its way into Mike's hide, Demaret, actually Hogan's best friend, would say such things as: "Don't pay any attention to him, Mike, he's just trying to get your goat." The more Hogan would shun Parco, the more Demaret would try to be Mike's friend. By the end of the round, Parco didn't know where he stood but he knew that he wasn't leader anymore—not with an eighty for the third round.

Hogan and Porky Oliver went on to tie for the title after seventy-two holes. The following day they staged an eighteen-hole play-off, and Oliver socked in with a one under seventy-one and lost by seven shots. That's right, "Little Mr. Legree" scorched the Porker with a sixty-four for all of the marbles.

That night Ben Hogan dined alone at the Chez Ami, which was the top nightclub of its time in our parts. Hogan, in those years, always dined alone. So when I walked in and saw him sitting there, the cynosure of all eyes, I walked over and asked him if he would like company. He amazed me as he stood up and asked me to sit down—I guess I thought he was made of metal. We had just a casual acquaintance (I'd interviewed him during the tourney), but you would have thought I was a long-forgotten, and suddenly sweetly remembered, friend from Texas. We chatted and we ate and we seemed to enjoy each other. Delighted at this turn of events, I said to Hogan, "Why is it that you can be so delightful here and such an entirely different and far from enjoyable individual while you are competing?" Hogan smiled that little smile that someone once, and so aptly, described as "having about as much mirth to it as a baby's gas pain," and said, "You look at my physique and at the way the other guys are built and you can understand why I must make up for it in extra concentration. That golf course is my office every single minute I'm playing in a tournament. If you are a businessman," continued Hogan, "and I come into your office, we talk business. We don't gab and laugh and wink and horse around. And when business is through, I get out of there. When I play golf, it is my business to win because that's the way I make a living and if I don't win I don't eat. If I win a lot, and I win a lot, then I eat well." It was the man's philosophy, and though I heartily disagreed with it at least it was his and I did ask the question in the first place, didn't I?

It wasn't more than a couple of years later that the news wires, full of the near-fatal accident in Texas, screamed "BEN HOGAN NARROWLY ESCAPES DEATH IN CAR CRASH IN TEXAS."

The details are history: An oncoming truck forced the Hogan car off the road. Just before the impact, Ben flung his body across that of his wife, Valerie, and saved her from almost certain death. So broken, so almost completely destroyed was Hogan's body that doctors predicted that Ben would never walk and, naturally, never play golf again. But men with the dedication and desire of a Hogan are not cut from the normal mold. Months of mending and then months of painful therapy and recuperation were in store for this man whose return to society and thence to the first tee were so dramatic that a movie was made of his life which enabled the world to know the determination of one of the greatest athletes of all time. Yet not even the movie could dig deeply enough into the being of Ben Hogan to tell of the almost miraculous transition that took place in him, the man. During his agonizing months of mental and physical frustration, when it appeared many times that the doctors might have been right, the world responded. His doctors were some of the very people that he regarded as only put on earth to pay to watch him play golf. He found out, as thousands have found out, that people, and people alone, are what make the world turn. Thousands upon thousands of letters, cards, telegrams, and greetings of every nature and from all ports of call, arrived in never-ending cascades of affection, of sympathy, and, yes, even of tolerance for a man who had been so intolerant of others for so long.

Slowly, as his strength returned, his basic qualities of a champion, which were so obvious in actual combat, began to infiltrate his heart as well as his mind. They said he would never walk or play golf again. He walked, and as for playing golf he returned and won every single major championship just to prove them wrong. But along the way he also proved the millions of his unknown and unseen well-wishers right. He learned to smile (and not as a gassy baby smiles) as he became human.

He came back to Buffalo after his long hours of darkness and his own deep, rewarding look at himself. When I left him this time, I felt that he was just a trifle bit sad for having missed so much of the humanness of his life. Yet, as he walked away, I also felt that he was infinitely happy, for he had learned compassion.

Konsek and Hogan—men to remember.

LEFTY GOMEZ

Lefty Gomez, the great Yankee pitcher of the great Yankee years, became one of the most sought-after banquet speakers in all of sports. His sense of humor, his brilliance at making himself the butt of the jokes by reflecting himself in the light of a dumb bunny, literally ravaged his audiences and left them gasping in their convulsions. Also, and this is the most important part of it, Lefty Gomez always left his audiences wanting more. We became warm friends, and we appeared many, many times together on the circuit here in western New York.

One of the outstanding banquets of the calendar year is the Buffalo Athletic Club sports night where some seven hundred men gather each November. Down through the years they have been treated to elegant elbow rubbing with every sports personality worth his salt and a few who moved in because they had friends on the committee. All hands knew the importance of an invitation to grace the BAC's sports night head table, and it was my pleasure to serve as master of ceremonies some seven times during the years. One year the event, after shining brightly for many years, suddenly began to pall. There was no lessening of attendance, for it was a command performance for audience as well as participant, but it just seemed to lose its luster. One day I was invited to MC the dinner. In a second I realized that what was wrong with the proceedings and what was becoming a deterrent to its continued success was its cumbersomeness.

I knew I could revitalize the dinner if given the chance, and when I told the committee that I would serve as its helmsman on the condition that I be allowed to conduct the speaking program in my own fashion they rather hesitatingly agreed. What hadn't occurred to them, but what should have because it was obvious to the poor souls at the speaker's table, was the length of time from invocation to benediction. Just the year before, the guest of honor, or mopup speaker, hit the mike exactly two and a half hours after the actual devouring of the dinner had been accomplished. He spoke to a half-empty hall and to a half-asleep yet astoundingly courteous audience. It was one of the few times I can remember when embarrassment could be audible. So, when invited to serve the following year, I vowed that, with dinner starting at seven, all hands would be on their way home, or back to the bar, by 10 P.M. sharp.

That particular night they handed me a list of eleven speakers and fourteen others who were only to be introduced. Lady Luck was riding at my shoulder as usual, for the main attraction was none other than Mr. Gomez. What I did was simple. A cocktail party was tendered for the visiting dignitaries, and while this was in progress I asked each of the men scheduled to talk to join with me in a private room. When I had collected my trained seals, I introduced myself to eleven household sports bywords and said, in essence, that I was happy to be with them and delighted they would share the evening with all of us. Then I told them, point blank, that I wanted each one to give me the best three-minute talk he could deliver. Not four minutes, not even three and a half minutes, but three minutes on the nose. Gomez, as main man, was allotted fifteen minutes.

Nothing ever worked more smoothly, and when fourteen men had been introduced and ten more had spoken, Gomez hit the mike twelve minutes before 10 P.M. He wowed them, he convulsed them, and then he shook them up. At thirty seconds before ten, by my watch, he stopped suddenly. He said; "This MC should change his name to Simon Legree. Thanks for allowing me to be your guest and good night." There was a stunned silence. Then, quietly, there was the benediction. At 10 P.M., the party adjourned. Gomez came up to me at the post-party binge, and I knew I had made a new friend. He said, "Five men have come up to me in the last ten minutes and said they wished I had gone on. They will be the first five men who will suggest one day that I be invited again. You always leave them wanting more just as a pitcher never gives any batter a full look at his entire bag of tricks." Lefty Gomez was invited back every year after that and accepted the invitations three times.

JACKIE ROBINSON

One day in 1946, I was sitting in the press box at Buffalo's Offerman Stadium before a game between the Buffalo and Montreal baseball clubs. It was a routine affair with neither team exceptionally outstanding but with excitement running high because temperatures rose and fevers flamed every time the Royals of Montreal came to grips with the Bison of Buffalo.

On this day in that year the public-address announcer, the storied Joe Deluhery, briefed the fans on the starting lineups with just a little extra emphasis on the name of the second baseman for Montreal. His name was Jackie Robinson, not an unusual tag in the United States, and he was a master of the art of defense and, at the proper time, of making pitchers wish they had been saved for some future foe. What distinguished Jackie Robinson from the majority of others was that he was black in a game that was so white at that time that no black man had ever worn the spangles of a major-league team.

As Jackie Robinson changed the complexion of so many minor baseball game results with his stellar glove and utterly destructive bat, so too did this man break the color monopoly by blazing on the major scene in 1947 as a member of the Brooklyn Dodgers. It was the celebrated Branch Rickey who took what many considered to be, at least at that time, one of the most potentially hazardous steps in the history of baseball. But wise old Rickey knew his product, and Jackie Robinson, realizing the historic part he played in the drama, gave Rickey every right to believe that he had made one of the wisest decisions of them all.

Every person even remotely interested in spectator sports activity watched every single move this one-time U.C.L.A. football wonder made. Jackie Robinson was taunted in every park where Dodgers played and only because he was black—the first of his race to be granted the right, which was his inheritance because he was born to our flag which was his flag as well, to play as a free man in a free world.

The man never answered even a single one of the invectives thrown his way. He was as great a player as any man who played the game and, as time passed, he was a greater man than many. He accepted his challenge with such a superb dignity that he shamed all who sought to shame him. The great second sacker, a tremendous fighter in every contest in which he played, carried his banner and the banner of his people high to the skies for the ten years that he blazed as one of the truly fine infielders of his time. And when his playing years were through and his waiting period had ended, he was hustled into the Hall of Fame at Cooperstown so fast that you had the feeling that those already enshrined couldn't wait until he arrived.

Someone once said of Joe Louis that he "laid a rose on Abraham Lincoln's grave." It could have been said of the pioneer baseballer, Jackie Robinson, for as the first black man to play under baseball's big top he proved himself the equal of any man who ever played the game. But more than anything else, Robinson issued a challenge to every single member of his race who was to follow him in the swift years ahead. He told them, by his deeds on the field of friendly strife and by his words and conduct in the course of everyday living, that there was a world open to them, as it was open to him when Branch Rickey decided that the time to break the color barrier was right.

Jackie Robinson was one of the truly great sports heroes of all time and thus will he ever be remembered. Yes, I remember Jackie Robinson from that first day in 1946 as I sat and called the plays in Offerman Stadium. That day I became his fan and I was one of the fortunate ones who reported his playing magic during his years. When his career ended, I never thought of him as either black or white. It didn't make any difference. It never has, but if the memory of Jackie Robinson calls for a color, then and by all means make it red, white, and blue. He was a distinguished American and a great athlete. Thus will he be remembered, thus will he be revered.

JESSE OWENS

During my three years at WBNY, I was brought face to face with the fact that anything can happen, anything at all, in this vale of tears we call a world. And what happened to me as I was battling to rid myself of the cloak of obscurity, one morning during the summer of 1936, was an experience that made me a firm believer in fate. Even its retelling still has an aura of the unreal about it, because when have you ever heard of a man with one of the most famous names in sports greeting another man who could easily have been considered the most anonymous individual in the same world at the time?

The year 1936 was an Olympic year and, by coincidence, the summer games were staged in Germany although the locale was Berlin and not, as in 1972, Munich. Of major importance to the United States was Jesse Owens, the world's greatest sprinter and quite naturally the main bulwark of the U.S. Olympic track and field aggregation.

Owens, the Columbus Comet from Ohio State, won the 100- and 200-meter dashes, the broad (long) jump, and anchored the 400-meter relay team. He gathered four gold medals to be placed in a treasured trophy case that must be as large as any other such receptacle in the world. When Owens was walking toward the spot where he was to receive his accolade, Adolf Hitler showed his class by rudely turning his heel and walking away before Jesse could catch up to him. What the reporters tried to turn into a world incident was simply shrugged off by Owens after the ceremony. To put an end to the whole thing, Jesse said, without batting an eye, "I came to run for Uncle Sam and not to meet Hitler."

When the games concluded, it was decided that a team would tour Europe before heading back to the United States and a ticker-tape parade down Broadway. It wasn't a matter of asking the athletes to join the group, it was to have been a command performance and it included Owens. But Owens, feeling that he had made his contribution, was having no part of it. He was weary, but more than that he was anxious to hurry on home and see his first born—an individual who strolled in while his Pop was strolling for medals in Berlin. Owens told the men that he was going home, and they said that if he did he would be suspended. A rather decent gesture of thanks for services rendered, don't you think?

Just about an hour later, Jesse Owens disappeared. He simply

101

vanished from the scene and no amount of detective work, snooping, tracing, or crystal gazing could establish his whereabouts. The world should have known that the most difficult thing of all in 1936 was catching up to Jesse Owens.

Our scene shifts from Berlin to Buffalo. About two weeks after Jesse's fadeout, a friend of mine called me at WBNY and handed it to me straight. "How," he asked, "would you like an interview with Jesse Owens?" My answer was, "How would you like to have lunch with Mary Pickford after she goes shopping with Douglas Fairbanks?" My friend, a patient man, said patiently, "If you would like to interview Jesse Owens say so, you bonzo, or we will go elsewhere." This guy wasn't one to spend idle moments tying up his friends' time in equally idle banter. So I said, "If you can have him at the studio in fifteen minutes, I'd be happy to interview Jesse Owens, or Jim Thorpe if he's with you, too."

Fifteen minutes later my friend came off the elevator on the sixth floor of the Nellany Building and if he wasn't accompanied by Jesse Owens then no imposter who ever lived was any more successful. As we dutifully shook hands, Owens was almost convulsed at my countenance, and said, "Small world, eh?" Right then it was such a small world that I only hoped they could find a grave big enough to plant me in. Yes, it was Jesse Owens all right. He had been able to give all hands the slip and had come into Buffalo during the night enroute to his home in Columbus and the reunion with his family. His appearance in the studio caused so much shock that the transmitter almost short-circuited, but thanks to the pleasantness and patience of Owens things finally were restored to normal.

That was about the longest interview I ever had, although what we said is of no part of my memory today. That wasn't important. What was important was that, against all odds, I happened to be the one to get the first interview with Owens upon his return to the States.

How remarkable was the man? How remarkable is the man today after giving a lifetime of dedicated devotion to youngsters the world over? Jesse comes back to Buffalo once or twice a year in the interests of the kids, and I feel certain that every time I see him he appears younger than when he stepped off that elevator. He once said, "When you travel the world and see it all, you come to only one conclusion: That our country has everything and that although it is interesting and educational to go to other lands, it is the most heartwarming thing on earth to come back to America at journey's end."

Would Jesse Owens, were he in his prime, win today? You have to say yes, for no one ever taught him to lose. And the man said it right when he said that America has everything. It was the only nation on earth who had the Comet from Columbus.

JOE LOUIS

Suddenly there burst upon the American sports scene a monster obliterator garbed in boxing trunks, a scowl that seemed to have been carved on his countenance, and the ability to hit with power that would have leveled any mule's kick to a gentle blow-by-breeze. Joe Louis wasn't black or white or red or green, he wasn't short or tall or fat or lean. He was every man, and he was basically America. And he was my friend. But I held no corner on that, for he was the friend of all people everywhere and he did more for his race, his sport, and the world in general, excluding Jackie Robinson, than ten other men could ever do in their lifetime—but Joe did it in the span of one boxing career.

After he and the world had been shocked into submission when Max Schmelling leveled Joe with fifty-six right-hand blows to the face (his only defeat when he was becoming ruler of the world's boxing roost), Louis became the finest fighting machine of his day. There has always been the suggestion, and we have walked this path before, that he was the greatest fighter of all time. But we have also concluded that there is no way to honestly and correctly define the greatest athlete in any category, so we'll let it go for what it's worth that Joe Louis was the master of all box fight men during his halcyon years. Many times was the question asked:

103

"Would Joe Louis have beaten Dempsey?" That evolved not so much into a question asked and argued wherever men gathered but it came close to erupting into a civil war. My answer, if not brilliant, at least was as good as any. Jack Dempsey could knock you out with a six-inch right hook. Joe Louis could knock you out with a six-inch left jab. Whichever got there first would have won.

Joe Louis came to Buffalo many, many times. After he was established as one of the great fighters, a Buffalo man by the name of Marshall Miles became Joe's manager. Miles, along with his brothers, ran the Vendome Hotel in our town and that was the general meeting place for all who went down to their sports in jabs, hooks, resin, and cauliflower ears. The mid-thirties also saw the western New York area as one of the strongest fistic citadels in the world with such fighters as Jimmy Slattery, Jimmy Goodrich, Rocky Kansas, Tommy Paul, George Nichols, Art Weigand, Freddie Mueller, and many other winners of countless titles and thousands of fights. We had one fellow who fought here prior to those years by the name of Willie ("KO") Brennan. Brennan never won a title, but he never left any doubt in any opponent's mind that he was a club fighter who came to box and not to play. His greatest boast was the fact—and it is an established fact—that he fought six opponents in six different cities in six consecutive nights and kayoed all six.

Louis never fought in Buffalo. He came here to relax and to confer with Miles, and he came here because he enjoyed the friendliness of our town and our area. He was the most willing man who ever laced on a glove when it came to taking time for interviews and he was also one of the most difficult to interview. Joe, despite his fabled fund of boxing equipment, was as taciturn as Calvin Coolidge. When he first came to stardom that vocabulary consisted of "yes" and "no," but as he polished his heavy artillery he became more conversant—although at career's end Joe Louis was still no conversationalist.

Yet that wasn't what Louis was put on this earth to be. Actually, I always thought of him as a symbol. More than that, I regarded him as native America in his tradition, in his strength, in his dedication to himself and to everyone else. In those early years, which must have been frightfully bewildering years for him, Joe Louis was just an underprivileged young man who had a God-given gift—the ability to whip a man, any man, within the confines of a boxing ring. That is where his accomplishments began and ended, and therefore anything foreign to fighting was alien to his comprehension. He was suckered by many men who sought to feed off him. And it wasn't until Marshall Miles came along and took a genuine interest in setting up defenses for Joe against a manipulating world that Louis actually began to live.

During the glory years for the Brown Bomber, he fought for the New York-based 20th Century Sporting Club. Long-time promoter Mike Jacobs was the man who was commander in chief of the Louis boxing program, and he knew a very, very good thing when he happened upon it. And Joe Louis was more than a good thing—he was solid gold in the bank. When Louis went into service in World War II, he was in need of ready cash but he knew that Jacobs would always advance as much money as he needed to enjoy life. As a consequence, when Joe's service hitch ended and he returned to the only thing he knew, box fighting, he was in debt to Jacobs to such an extent that he had to fight for Mike to pay him back. Toward the end of his career, Miles did the level best he could to try to straighten Joe out financially. Louis didn't quit broke, but he didn't retire, as he should have, wealthy to the point of independence in the dollar league, either.

Joe Louis loved to laugh and probably still does, although I am quite certain that he doesn't think much about life is funny anymore. But when he owned the world and was kicking heavyweights over as if he were bowling ten pins, life was just a great big game to be enjoyed to the fullest. He loved to rib and be ribbed, and many was the night when the gang would gather round here in town and trade banter with the then-super athlete of the athletic world.

One of Joe's easiest opponents was a character by the name of

Kingfish Levinsky. In his twilight, the Kingfish came to Buffalo for some reason, either to box a nobody or to referee, right after he had been stoned by Louis. The story that Louis knocked him out while the Kingfish was playing to the audience was only partly true, as he admitted during an interview he and I had one evening. "They say, Kingfish," I began, "that Louis knocked you out while you were looking out at the crowd. Is that true?" With a look of utter scorn, as if to suggest that simply looking at a boxing audience was strictly a waste of time, Levinsky answered, "Naw—who looks at a crowd? I was looking at a blonde."

Tony Galento, one of the most unbelievable characters that boxing ever foisted on an unsuspecting public, was the man, even more so than Billy Conn, who came close to upsetting the mighty Louis when Joe was at his very peak. Galento, famed as Two Ton Tony, came racing toward Louis as the bell sent the men into action in round one. He started a right from that corner, and it missed Joe's chin by the length of one of the hairs on that chin. Had it connected they'd have had to retrieve Louis's head, once it stopped rolling, out on Eighth Avenue. It was the same type of punch that the Bull of the Pampas, Luis Angel Firpo, actually landed on the unsuspecting Jack Dempsey and one that dumped Dempsey on his drawers outside of the ring. Only friendly and worried American newspapermen shouldered Jack back into the ring in time to beat the count and save the heavyweight crown for America when it seemed destined for Argentina.

The Louis confrontation with Conn, the overgrown middleweight, could have resulted in a Conn victory, and had Billy retained a small measure of common sense it would have. Billy was a fine boxer, and the night he met Joe Louis he had the Bomber so bewildered with his in-and-out, punch-and-run style of boxing that Joe resembled a frustrated, snorting, angry bull in the ring. Conn was a sheetful of points ahead of the champion when, evidently seduced by a feeling of false security, he got smart and whacked Louis on the chops. That was all right because that was what he was in there to do. But Billy made the mistake of laughing when he did it, and within one whiplash of a second Conn was

106

deadweight on the canvas—his dreams of conquest nothing but a thin layer of resin touching his back. That was it with Joe Louis. You knew it would come, but you never knew when.

Joe Louis came to greatness during my early years, when I was, in a smaller way, also fighting for recognition. Reporting him, even from afar, was a thrilling experience and a rewarding one because the way Louis fought and the way he lived brought out all of the potential skill in this young announcer. And a guy like Louis was tremendously important to any young reporter willing to learn because he made you study him as a fighter inside the ring and as a man outside. He did as much for his race as any athlete who ever lived. Yet he did it, not as a Negro in a predominantly white nation, but as an American from a humble beginning fighting to succeed in an America that has always recognized those who were willing to sacrifice and learn for the sake of future success.

If Joe Louis wasn't the greatest fighter who ever lived, and he could well have been, he was and he is as fine as any man who ever played any game, fought any foe, anywhere on earth.

CY WILLIAMS

One night in 1935, wrestling had taken over the old Broadway Auditorium and, as a young, skinny and bright-eyed neophyte reporter, I was there before anybody else. It was my first event, and I wasn't going to miss a thing. That evening two former football all-Americans, Len Macaluso from Colgate and Cy Williams from the University of Florida, were to do battle. They were wrestling for the title, said the promoter, although what title was never clarified. Maybe for the championship of Broadway and Michigan, on which corner the auditorium stood. To save you from the gory details, when it was all over Macaluso, apparently dead, lay prone on the canvas while Williams, frantically frustrated, seething with anger, was held in one corner of the square by four coppers. Macaluso was rushed to Emergency Hospital and Williams was ushered off to a cell on the third floor of the Erie County Jail.

When dawn of the following morning arrived, I was wrestling

bed sheets with hammerlocks, elbow smashes, and step-over-toe holds. My imagination was right on fire, and though my sympathy was for Macaluso, my heart belonged to Williams. After all, it *was* an accident, wasn't it? Wasn't it? So, unable to pin the sandman, I got dressed and beat it down to the jail. Nervous, as becomes the novice, I cleared my throat and croaked, "Mr. Williams, I'm sorry for what happened last night." Cy raised his eyes from the book he was reading and looked straight at me. Then his face softened and he asked, "Who are you? What's your name?" I told him my name and that I was a sportscaster. He asked, "How long have you been in this business?" "Five weeks, almost," I answered. He stood up and said, "Come here, Ralph."

Softly did Cy Williams speak. "We wrestlers would rather fight than eat. But because we and our families have to eat, we wrestle. Millions of people come to watch us, to enjoy it, and go away from the performance willing to spread the good word about wrestling." Cy paused, and you knew he was having a ball. Then he resumed. "No, we don't talk about wrestling and we enjoy it, but I am going to do you a favor, Ralph (if he'd called me Ralphie I would have cried right there), because you have shown that you are a young man of great compassion to worry because something happened to me. Maybe I can put you and your career a little ahead of yourself by telling you that tomorrow night in Syracuse I go to the hospital and he goes to jail."

MA MILLER

Ma Miller shuffled her way into my life during the early fifties when Chuck Healy and I were televising the wrestling matches from Memorial Auditorium. By then I had moved from WGR to WBEN which had studios high up in the Statler Hilton Hotel.

One evening, as usual after my 6:15 sportscast, I returned to my office to file my script prior to the trip home for dinner. The reception room was empty save for a little old lady whom I noticed as I sped back to the office. She stood almost up to my chest bone and she was ageless after the manner of a person who has lived a long lifetime. She wore thick, so very thick, glasses which lay so far down on her nose that you didn't believe she was getting any use out of them at all and were amazed that they nose-stuck at all. She had on a black hat which appeared to be older than she, a frayed coat and a dress that never could have had any color to it. This lady carried an umbrella and a tremendous purse that was, undoubtedly, her home away from home, or perhaps the only home she had.

She was squarely placed in front of me when suddenly the whole place lit up because the lady smiled although if she had teeth she must have left them home. But she had a twinkle in her eyes and she had merriment in her laughter and youth, tapping some hidden resource I guess, in the voice that announced: "Ralphie—I'm Ma Miller. How about a ticket to the wrestling matches tonight?" Had she said: "How about waltzing to the moon with me, Ralphie?" I wouldn't have been more shocked and I can tell you, that once we became friends, I would have waltzed with her to the moon and made a little history a lot earlier than it was actually made and with a lot less expense. Ma Miller was the only person who ever called me Ralphie and got away with it and she didn't look to be the wrestling type but I fell in love with her at first glance and she could have had a ticket to Paradise if I'd had one handy.

As I reached for a ticket (wrestling) we headed for the elevator. Once aboard she laid down the ground rules 'cause this wasn't just a one night stand for Ma—this was from here to eternity. She said: "In the future I will meet you in the same place and you can give me a ticket each week. But that will be on Wednesday. On Friday, when you and Chuckie drive to the matches, I will be in front of the Statler." There was no hint of a request in her voice. This was the captain telling the troops how to proceed. For almost five years she kept her time charts and we followed her instructions—you had better believe.

Ma knew all about my family and alluded, in a sort of vague, reminiscent way, to hers. She knew all there was to know about wrestling and she knew that Gotch and Hackenschmidt were two of the greats of early wrestling and not a German law firm. Wednesday the ticket, Friday the taxi, without meter, every Wednesday and every Friday. Then, one Wednesday she didn't come for the ticket and on Friday she wasn't in front of the Statler for the ride when Chuckie and Ralphie drove up. Days and weeks went by and no Ma Miller. Then, one day, a pathetic little note told us that she was ill in Meyer Memorial Hospital. We hot footed it to that mansion of mercy and we found her—littler, infinitely older. But when we walked to her bed and she opened her eyes it was as if a new day had dawned. That great, toothless smile and that crackly laughter were followed by, "Here are my boys, I told you they would come." The whole ward buzzed and Ma was in her glory for what she had boasted to her friends was, in fact, the truth. Her boys were those television fellas, Chuckie and Ralphie.

From time to time we called on her and the last time we called, her bed was empty. We weren't surprised, just saddened no end, to hear that, one night, Ma Miller had slipped away to shed the weight of her little world that must have been a heavy burden at best. Ma left us both better men for having known her. She taught us the meaning of courage by proving that it was her greatest stock in trade.

As I walked out, that day, I recall thinking that she had slipped back to the bosom of her God tired and willing after 91 years of fighting to live. Chuck and I feel today that she didn't live entirely alone and that, maybe at the end, she felt her fellas beside her.

JOHN C. STIGLMEIER

The year 1904 was important to the next Hubbell Hall of Famer, who has served as one of the bulwarks in my life. That was the year that John C. Stiglmeier became a blacksmith. The smithy shop was at 314 Seneca Street in Buffalo, and although Stiggy wasn't destined to shoe horses for the rest of his life he was hard at the trade long enough to resemble a blacksmith. And if you could see him today, as he marches brightly through his eighties, you'd say he is still a smithy. John Stiglmeier still stands straight and tall, and he has the clipped hair and the muscles to spare that become anyone's mind picture of a blacksmith.

After Stiggy's years of singing in the anvil chorus, he turned to a less rigorous and far more rewarding life. There is little question but that a good blacksmith is a talented and valuable man. But he doesn't come in contact with too many people plying that trade, and horses aren't in the habit of conversing—although they'll give you a laugh now and then. Thus did the man Stiglmeier, who enjoyed people as few men ever have, start moving into the sunlight and among men. In 1917, John became mayor of the village of Depew—a suburb of Buffalo—and he ruled the community in which he still resides with affection and meaning. In 1931, the very year my needle scratched, Stiglmeier stepped down as chief executive of Depew and devoted his time to private business.

The foregoing could easily be the full story of a man's life if you followed it to its gentle, quiet, and rewarding conclusion. That, however, is not the saga of John C. Stiglmeier. While he was Hizzoner of Depew, Stiggy entered the field of professional baseball and gave more to it in every way than any man ever even came close to giving. In 1922, Stiggy entered the Buffalo International League baseball picture as general manager. Save for a three-year period, he stayed with it until the razing of Offerman Stadium broke his heart. He retired from the administrative part of baseball in 1963, after forty-one years of hard work trying to give Buffalo the best baseball outside of the majors that he could. Immediately after John stepped out of the scene baseball's light began to flicker, and that flame blew itself out completely just a short while later. Professional baseball will never return to Buffalo until a decent, accredited stadium is built to house it. And this is not one man's opinion. It is a decree as set forth by the fathers of major-league baseball who, realizing the tremendous potential of

111

this area for the activity, have added ". . . and once that stadium is constructed, the franchise will be in the mail."

That is for the future to decide and for a future historian to chronicle. My pleasant task is to recreate Stiglmeier as we knew him. Surely I could do better if I had a piece of solid granite and a chisel with which to depict this man of strength. But I would not be getting the job done right by just constructing the exterior of this giant who moved so gently among us and still does today. You can't carve a heart out of granite. And great as was this man's physique, his heart was greater.

There were two strokes of good fortune for me when I first began spieling for a living. The first was when, in the very first month of my broadcasting, I met Stiggy. The second was when he gave visable evidence that he liked me. John judged you by your willingness and your ability to learn. He could understand ineptness if it was accredited to inexperience. But he had absolutely no interest in, nor anything further to do with, a person who did not think that there is always more to learn and that no man, even at his journey's end, is truly complete. Attitude toward yourself, toward all others, toward life itself—that is what keeps a man thinking young while his wisdom is tempered by experience as he totals counted years he cannot escape. That's the way Stiggy felt, and because he did those of us who came under his guidance and who felt his loyalty many times in many ways were taught the same philosophy. Joe McCarthy lives his life thinking in those terms, Tem did, Stiggy still does, and so do I as I am certain that thousands of you beyond the covers of this book do.

Applying this philosophy to his daily contacts with players, coaches, managers, trainers, and the fans gave John a stature most men never reach. So many times, after one of his boys would move to the majors, would he return to Stiggy for counsel if the way suddenly became rutted. Not in matters of baseball alone did this father to us all grant us the shoulder to cry on and advice when the answers were few. His office was never closed—and that went for his home on Wagner Avenue in Sloan as well.

112

The fact that so many great Buffalo players passed their major-league preparatory exams in Offerman Stadium under the guidance of Stiglmeier quite naturally meant that the majors wanted to find out about this man of whom these young men spoke so highly. In time they came to him, and in time they gave him their complete respect—and for good reason. This man was what baseball and every other sport needs most of all—a strong, fair, honest, and fearless individual. In Stiggy, they received a four for one bargain. Shag Shaughnessy, long-time president of the International League, George Trautman, czar of all of the minor circuits, Ford Frick, and Will Harridge regarded Stiglmeier as necessary to the success of baseball administration. Ray Schalk, former Bison manager and one of the greatest catchers of all time, wouldn't move without talking with Stiggy, and Schalk and Joe McCarthy specifically requested John to go with them when they checked into their rooms at baseball's Hall of Fame. Stiggy was named baseball administrator of the year by the *Sporting News*—in 1944 and again in 1959.

In short, and not to belabor a point, John Stiglmeier conducted his baseball business as administrative head of the Buffalo team but all of baseball kept tabs on him. And he kept tabs on his friends. Stiggy never liked to travel alone. One year, the International League staged a meeting in Miami to discuss the inclusion of Havana. By coincidence, the Orange Bowl game was to be played there at the same time. So Stiggy called me and said, "Be at my house at seven tomorrow because we're flying to Miami." And we had a ball.

That was John during his extended years of devotion to this area of western New York. He was so important to professional baseball that on several occasions he could have ventured into major soil and harvested a banner crop. But he, as with the guy with whom you are walking, had that peculiar dedication to this countryside right here that motivated his desire to start here, remain here, and live out his years here. John and Mame, his wife, are fine today and neither has lost that effervescence that both must

113

have found together in their long ago. John C. Stiglmeier—a mighty smithy—was as mighty of heart as of hand.

Succeeding generations weary of a remark such as, "They just don't make 'em the way they used to anymore." This is in reference to some individual back then whose durability was so fibrous as to brook no comparison with anyone who followed after. John Stiglmeier would be the last to say that he was more bemuscled and hewn from a stronger oak than any other man but, in truth, he was.

An incident came to light just the other day when the now 86-year-old one-time blacksmith noticed a nagging ache at the base of his spine. It seems that in 1934, riding in a car with his bosom buddy, Ray Schalk, an accident befell the twosome in the nature of a two-car crackup. The impact was so tremendous that Stiggy was lifted right up through the roof. He suffered a bruised back, and at that time, and with no x-ray ordered, it was said that he had injured the sciatic nerve. Some ten days later, John was up and walking again, and through the years his back bothered him only occasionally.

Then came the other day when the nagging ache and an ultimate visit to his doctor were in order. John told his physician about the back incident in 1934, and when the doctor suggested an x-ray, Stiggy demured but not to any great extent. Two days later, our hero received a call from the doctor who said he wanted to see him in his office, pronto. The still swiftly moving octogenarian responded and was severely castigated by the doctor for not revealing the true nature of his injury which had been suffered thirty-eight years ago. "What do you mean true injury?" was John's reaction. "I mean," said the doctor, "that your x-rays show that you didn't just bruise your back or injure your sciatic nerve in 1934. Mr. Stiglmeier, your back was broken." And what did the smithy say? He said, "You brought me all the way into your office just to tell me that?"

No, dear friend, they don't make 'em the way they used to anymore.

FREDDY HUNT

Frederick Tennyson Hunt, Sr., is his name and playing, coaching, and administering hockey is his fame.

Freddy Hunt was born in Brantford, Ontario, a long time ago. When you are a boy child in Canada, you teethe on the blade of a hockey stick because, as the U.S.S.R. found out, hockey in Canada is not a sport—it is a dedicated way of life. Although Hunt never actually told me so, it has always been obvious that from the time he was old enough to distinguish between a red line and a blue line he never thought of anything else except hockey. And when he served his apprenticeship and distinguished himself through the normal processes of the Canadian amateur ranks, he stood qualified and ready for a place in the professional sun.

Though he played in NHL competition for a brief spell and sparkled as a tremendous stick handler, back checker, and goal scorer in the American League, I never felt that his forte was playing the game. Nor did I feel that Hunt was particularly interested in the coaching aspect of professional hockey. Freddy proved this particular contention of mine right by stepping in as an interim coach in the Buffalo situation one season, and, as quickly, stepping out again.

No, my wager on Fred Hunt would be what it ultimately became, a prognostication of administrative success in a world that, once it started to develop, grew with such rapidity that even today, with the World Hockey Association posing such competition for the NHL, hockey is making envious eyes at other activities which do not relish competition. Baseball, football, and basketball have always been the top kicks in the American competitive sports scene. Now their ranks have been invaded by hockey, and this upstart has no intention of staying at one level when it has world dominance within its grasp.

This is the picture which frames the gentle Hunt. And it is not a come-lately position for Fred. When his playing days with the Buffalo Bison team were through, and when his great wife, Sis,

115

wearied of his several retirements and finally made him stick to one, Hunt became the general manager of the Buffalo team and served in that position, and with tremendous success, for the ensuing eighteen years or, until 1970, when the victorious years for Buffalo ended as this city's hockey future found a new refrigerator, the National Hockey League.

When the Bison aggregation went into the discard to make room for major competition, the Hunt-integrated club was the fiercest, most able team in the entire realm of the minor league. But the Knox brothers had long fought to earn expansion prominence for this, their native heath, and, though it cost them dearly, their battle was rewarded when Buffalo traded the best of minor activity for, and temporarily we hope, the worst of major hockey. That is not a castigation—it is merely a statement of fact. One of the curses of growing to major proportions is that growth is not a sudden thing. It is a long, hard, dog-eat-dog, and frustrating road, as the Buffalo Sabres and other expansion clubs are finding out. The National Hockey League wants you in, wants your money (and they judge it by the millions), and wants all it can get without giving you a thing except a place to absorb beating after beating. Then, when you have fought the good fight, the agonizing fight, you begin to win a few, and in time you start to win more than you lose.

Buffalo and the Knox brothers were fortunate that the Sabres came into being with the strength of the Bisons and that the proximity to Canada and the fact that Toronto's Maple Leaf Gardens are automatic sellouts for years to come insured full houses. In this instance, then, Canadians from Hamilton, St. Catherines, Fort Erie, and other way stations can see their national pastime in Buffalo. And they were the quickest to respond when the season sale was first advertised. The Knox men dreamed their initial dream some six years before they finally were able to ice a team in the National Hockey League. Had it not been for their great knowledge of and adherence to building on solid, well-organized, correctly staffed foundations, no part of this dream

116

could have escaped becoming a horrendous nightmare. But they had learned all of this years ago, and so, too, had David Forman, who is actually the man with his finger on every pulse of the organization. You learn by doing, of course, but when you start the rough road to establishing your community as an entity in the mad world of major sports activity you need perserverance, know-how, and money—not just a lot of money, but bales of money and preferably thousand-dollar bills in bales. There is no way possible for Americans and Canadians to evaluate the gratitude they feel for what the Knox brothers have contributed to the joy of their existence.

The slight detour from the man Hunt is understandable, I believe, for it gives me this chance to give you the details relative to the solid-gold hockey situation in this area. The foundation for what one day is hoped will be a tenacious NHL proving ground was not something that was laid overnight. It started in those war years when Eddy Shore brought his Springfield franchise here and then took his Indians back to Massachusetts, and it continued through to the mid-fifties when the Pastor brothers, of Pepsi-Cola fame, poured their money and their dedication into the franchise and made it a first-class enterprise. It came to full stature in the sixties, as its success merited the greatest attendance totals, year after year, in minor-league hockey. And through every single phase of its life, the Buffalo Hockey Club knew the wisdom and the strength of Freddy Hunt—the only man who was a part of every step of its growth.

The Hunt–Hubbell relationship started the very first time we ever met. When Freddy Hunt, Jr., and Susie Hunt came along to make the Hunt clan a foursome, Ann and I were deeply flattered to be asked to serve as their godparents. In times of sickness and strife, and in times of health and good fellowship and daily living, there has always been a warm feeling of two families living a kind of co-existence. This spans a matter of thirty years. A friendship, and I say it proudly, that no amount of time can ever weaken.

The Sabre reins are ably held by Punch Imlach as the general manager and by Floyd Smith as the team coach. But the assistant general manager, the man best qualified to serve in any capacity in the event the situation calls for emergency measures, is the same man who has always been the most important part of the Buffalo hockey picture—Frederick Tennyson Hunt, Sr., the poet of the ice—and one of the finest friends I've ever had. One of my proudest moments was when Fred became an American citizen and I stood by his side.

SUGAR RAY ROBINSON

Sugar Ray Robinson, the elegant clarinet of the ring, and Freddy Hutchinson never met. Yet they had one common denominator—the desire to win. It was as strong and consuming in one as in the other, and it is a quality, I am certain, that distinguishes the great athlete from the good athlete. The pity of it is that all men who play games don't go to their arenas toting total desire with which to parlay their athletic genius. Maybe that's why racing has win, place, and show.

The first time I ever set eyes upon Sugar Ray Robinson was when he looked like a dancing spindle at the age of seventeen. It was back in the old auditorium days, and the little whirling swizzle stick was the hit of an amateur boxing show. Right then, Robinson, a complete unknown, could have been had for the taking but the local boxing gentry simply let him get away. And what got away—became—what many experts who know far more about boxing than I consider possibly the greatest fighter, pound for pound, who ever darted through the ring ropes. And if Buffalo didn't want him, or didn't recognize his potential, you can wager it all that New York did and that's where Ray went. He came under the kindly guidance and faultless wisdom of a man by the name of George Gainsford. The man and the boy developed a lasting affection, one for the other. The man taught the boy everything he knew about the art of fisticuffing but, at that, he didn't need to teach Robinson much. For this youngster was born to fight, and he was born with that built-in instinct that, along with desire, sets the champions apart from the pack.

What Gainsford gave to Ray was discipline, rigid discipline. George knew that he had a genius on his hands, and he knew, as well, that the impatience of youth can be extremely costly. So, in his endless teachings, George Gainsford taught Ray Robinson his most important lesson: Fight when you are ready to fight and not a round before. Ultimately, when Robbie was properly groomed, polished, and frustrated by the lack of competition, Gainsford turned him loose and the little dancing fellow never looked back. Not long ago I saw Ray on one of the variety talk shows, and he still appears as if he could go in any ring with any man and walk away unmarked. For you can't mark, and therefore you can't knock out a man you cannot hit. That seemed to be the toughest of all trick's for Ray's opponents, and it must have been the most infuriating emotion—seeing the smiling countenance of a man you'd like to punch out of your county yet can't even lessen the smile on his face because you can't touch his face. Robbie's mastery of his boxing art was a sight to behold because, as with Muhammed Ali, Robinson could do it all. He had speed that was incredible—speed with his hands, speed in his foot motion, speed in his attack, speed in his sudden shift in defensive tactics which suddenly found him back on the attack again. As with Hank Armstrong, Ray Robinson stayed busy, busy, busy. But, unlike Armstrong, whose style didn't really require it, Ray had the perfect defenses.

There was another similarity between Robinson and Armstrong. Each won three divisional world titles. The only difference was that Hank held his simultaneously whereas Ray, who won the lightweight, welterweight, and middleweight crowns, held his at separate times. How would these men do today? Sorry, friend, I must beg off. I don't live in the past with the greats of those years, I simply visit there, remember them, and then come quickly back to the present where my attitude reminds me to do what I have always done—look forward.

Robinson always liked Buffalo, and as a result fought here many times. He was the friendliest guy in the world and was easily one of the truly fun interviews out of the hundreds of men with

119

whom I chatted during the magic microphone years. During the WBEN chapter in the Statler-Hilton, our studios were on the eighteenth floor. This posed a problem for Ray because he had, and I imagine still has, a real fear of elevators. This claustrophobia-type affliction meant, simply, that if he were to be interviewed, he'd have to walk up to that eighteenth plateau. What Ray did was to take a room on the tenth floor. He'd walk from the lobby to his room, and then when the time for broadcasting arrived he'd walk to the top. I say walk—actually he ran up and he ran down for he was a conditioning bug and he was also loaded with enough energy to motivate those Statler elevators.

The last time that Robinson fought here, he took on Henry Brimm, a good fighter, and a fellow who, I recall, held Robbie to a draw that night. Before heading for the battle pit, Ray came sprinting up to the studios for an air visit. I recall it vividly because it was the last time I ever chatted with him. During the course of that interview—and you must remember that Ray was closing in on his fistic farewell—the Sugar Kid startled me and my listeners with the announcement that, after the Brimm fight, he was retiring. My reaction must have been more than slightly skeptical, for the smiling fellow suddenly became serious as he said, "That's the truth, Ralph, this is going to be it. And if I ever fight again I'll walk back to Buffalo from wherever I happen to be and run up the Statler stairs just to apologize."

That was a parcel of years ago. Ray Robinson did fight again and didn't walk back to Buffalo to personally deliver an apology which I didn't want. When an athlete tells you, while he's still able and healthy, that he is going to retire, you can know for certain that his intention is to retire but his moment of truth comes when he asks himself, "So where do I go from here?" A man, especially an athlete, uses his best learning and productive years playing games for money. When he quits, he is lost because he hasn't developed any other talent—and therefore any other means of making a living. Robinson tried business ventures and personal appearances. But he wasn't a business man and he was just a fair hoofer.

But he was one of the greatest of all boxing champions. Thus he went back to boxing, because that was all he knew, and they never come back. And he knows that now.

TED WILLIAMS

In 1951, I developed a tubercular cavity in one lung and a month later I was ensconced in the Niagara Sanatorium in Lockport, New York. All people at the San were kindred spirits, all were suffering from the same disease. You felt their compassion and their support, and you knew, as you were allowed to become a member of the team, that this victory could be achieved. Our medical captain was Leonard Evander, a most remarkable man. After ten months of every known type of therapy, Dr. Evander came in one day and said that only thoracic surgery would do the trick. A lobectomy with a wedge resection was performed in February 1952, and the road back was a pleasant one. And the day I returned to my desk and my mike was one of thanksgiving, you had better believe.

Of my life at the sanatorium one of my most vivid memories is of Walter Drozdowski.

Droz was admitted to Niagara Sanatorium in 1942 with possibly the slimmest chance for a month's survival of any person who ever went to that great mansion of mercy. To give you only a slight idea of the courage and the determination of one man, I tell you, in truth, that Droz died nineteen years later and with a smile on his lips.

There were many reasons why this individual didn't accept the original prognosis of "death at any time." The best, of course, was that he didn't want to die and outlived the prediction to prove it. One of the true reasons for living for Droz was so he could go on hating the New York Yankees and loving, as closely as a man can love an unknown idol, Ted Williams—the master of the art of hitting a baseball. Walt simply could not stomach a Yankee victory. He so loathed the club (while I was there, and I loved the Yanks, they were tough tyrants of the baseball world) that he

121

formed what he called the "I Hate the Yankees Club." He talked every male in the sanitorium, and a few females as well, into joining. All except Hub. So well did Droz marshal his forces and so aptly did he integrate his hate with his membership that I had a game-by-game dollar wager on the Yanks with each member of the IHYC. Each afternoon, about five, there would be a single-file procession into Room 323 for the purpose of depositing one buck on the foot of my bed. My gracious thanks were parlayed with my exhortation to all members to keep hating the Yanks, and thus keep supporting the coffers of the Hubbell clan. Those were sunny afternoons and such things as streptomycin, pneumo, P.A.S., and x-rays were briefly shunted to the background.

Walt Drozdowski's obvious feeling against the Yanks, deep-rooted as it appeared to be, couldn't come close to what he felt for Ted Williams in intensity. Hate doesn't shine as affection shines, and when I say that Droz had himself an idol in Williams I could easily be making the understatement of the century. His room was a living William's shrine, and you almost felt at times that somewhere, Ted could sense this adoration from a sickly man who was wasted to swizzle-stick proportions.

One day, as often happened to this fellow who always was the first to donate himself as a guinea pig for a new TB drug or type of surgery (he wanted so much to live), Dr. Evander came into my room and said that Droz had suffered a bad coughing spasm. Later in the evening it was obvious that the little guy was going to have a rough time if he hoped to make it this time. The doctor said, "I think he can go through the night and maybe through tomorrow. On that chance, let's see what we can do with Mr. Williams."

Boston had played a game in Yankee Stadium that day, so I got in touch with the hotel where the Red Sox were staying, and as part of the miracle found Ted in his room. In telling Williams Droz's story, I mentioned the fact that he was an avowed Yankee hater. That helped, I know, because the Yanks were never favorites of Williams either. Used to coming through when he was needed, this big guy of world fame moved into high gear, sending by air autographed pictures and baseballs and a bat, and he wrote Droz a letter. The gifts arrived the next day, and Droz, having made it through the night, was awake when Dr. Evander walked in with them the next morning. As he entered the room, the Grim Reaper must have passed him on the way out, because once Walt Drozdowski fully understood, the look of despair faded and was replaced by a countenance of disbelief. As we stood there we witnessed a miracle.

In two days, Droz had thrown off whatever had bugged him, and the following day he appeared to be his old self. Only this time he was the king of the third floor. He sat, not in a hospital room, but in a room fit for a king with his Williams treasures grouped around him. Who knows, outside of Him, if Droz lived through his siege because of Williams' attentiveness and compassion and quick thinking? None of us really sought that answer. The experience had proved the class and decency of an often-maligned super athlete, and it confirmed our belief in the inner strength of Walt Drozdowski. The afternoon that Droz was first cognizant of his gifts from Ted Williams, Boston shell-shocked the Yankees into defeat. Maybe that was what enabled Walt to keep on living—just so that he could go on detesting those Yankees.

HANK ARMSTRONG

Hank Armstrong was the only man to hold and successfully defend three world boxing championships at the same time. He won the featherweight, the lightweight, and then the welterweight titles, and then rested his case. Such a feat would be impossible today, for you forsake one title when you win another.

There was a time when all fighters, thanks to the diligence of Charley Murray, our top promoter, stood in line to fight in this area. Thus it was no surprise when Armstrong, already the world's featherweight king, readily accepted a bout here. He knew that he would be matched with a good opponent, and he was certain, and this was more to the point, that he would be nationally spotlighted. He came here in 1936, and he became my friend. Actually, he

123

became more of a friend to Ann, who seemed to be a mother or sister confessor to so many of the athletes and characters we—a couple of characters ourselves—have met along the way. Strangely, boxing is the one sport that Ann couldn't care less about. As a matter of fact, it's one she, personally, is happy to see fade away. Thus the interest she had in Henry Armstrong was that of a friend more than an admirer of his fistic genius.

The mini-executioner was a startling individual to watch in action. He never stepped backward, and he never stood still. As a consequence, because of his superb physical condition and his lethal rights and lefts, the box-type individual had little or no chance with him because he allowed no fighter, ever, to get set. And woe be to the man who attempted to slug with him. Statistics have always been a bore to me, so I can't quote you his record. But I think most of it is filed in the top surgical wards of the hospitals of this nation. Not many of Henry's bouts went to decision. Not many of his opponents went straight home.

Just before Armstrong was to go to Pompton Lakes, New Jersey, to train for a title fight with Barney Ross—one of the true champions of all sports history—Hank was in Buffalo for a fight. In those years, Singers' Gym on Washington Street, sixty-seven steps above street level and in a building with no elevator, was the mecca of all of the maulers. Jack Singer, Sr., and Junior Singer, his son, hosted most of the greats.

One day, after Armstrong had finished off his activity, I waited for him to dress and we went out for a stroll, talking of many things. Hank wasn't ready to retire, but he was thinking of it because he had made a great deal of money and he knew, better than most, that his particular style of fighting, whereas it was devastating as long as the machine functioned with youth as one of its cogs, was no match for an early arrival of Father Time. "After the Ross fight, maybe I'll call it quits," said Hank. "But let's wait and see what happens when I fight Barney." Most of the world knew what was going to happen when the hammers were lowered on the aging chin of Mr. Rasofsky, but Armstrong wasn't buying

124

any part of complacency. "We'll know about Ross after the fight," was the way Hank put it. Then he said, "How about you and Mrs. Hubbell coming down to see the fight as my guests? Plan to come to Pompton Lakes and then, when I break camp, you can have a weekend in New York and watch the fight."

You can bet that we snapped up the invitation. We set sail right after I finished work one night and drove all night. We went to Pompton Lakes the next day, and you just never could have asked for a more generous host. Hank introduced us all around, and we elbowed with some of the great boxers and boxing writers of the era. Then we said farewell, and with a wish for luck we went on to New York where we never did see the fight. It had been scheduled for outdoors on the following Monday night, but rain came and the fight was postponed. Sadly did we haul ourselves back to Buffalo and settle for Don Dunphy's description—and no one ever described a fight quite so accurately or eloquently as did Dunphy. Maybe it was better that way, because Armstrong made a standing rib roast out of the hapless Ross and that was what Ann couldn't comprehend—not in the name of sport.

Not too long after that fight, Hank Armstrong retired, and as with most men who plied that trade it wasn't too long before he had gone through most of his earnings and savings. He turned to preaching, and the last I heard tell of him he was still spreading the word of the Lord.

JIM THORPE

In the twilight of his years, Jim Thorpe, the storied Carlyle Indian who did everything well and much of it better than most, toured the civilized world visiting with and counseling children. From time to time, his big brogans would walk the celebrated and massive Indian legend into our town, and we would never let one of his visits go by without seeking him out and putting a mike in front of him or, as we did in 1948, focusing a camera on his chiseled face.

Jim Thorpe actually resented being called, as he was so many

125

times, the greatest individual athlete of all time. And he was one of the first to make me conscious of how really unintelligent such a bland, all-encompassing, impossible-to-prove, and unnecessary statement that is. ''My track and football years,'' Jim Thorpe said, ''were early years when there were no true super stars. I was big and I knew how to play football and I could run and no one was any stronger. But that was back then. Today there are hundreds of better athletes than Thorpe ever was. It is just that there are so many today that it is difficult for one individual to stand out. In my years, they called me great because I could beat 'em all—but there weren't very many.'' He was very serious about it, and there was no phony aspect of playing himself down. He was great, he knew it, and he acknowledged it—but he was far from the greatest and he acknowledged that fact also.

Our meetings took place in two spots. One was the War Memorial auditorium during the wrestling T.V. hour on Friday. The second was at a local saloon where Chuck Healy, Hub, and Thorpe would go for a night-ending brew. Big Thorpe always delighted in being interviewed and in sitting with us during the wrestling commentary. He was always willing, and it must have been a tedious task at times, to sign his name for the never-ending line of autograph seekers and to answer every question that was put to him. But then that is the mark of greatness which sets the class athletes apart. They know the value of compassion and this means taking time for others. It was a simple philosophy of the man who walked with such meaning and such dignity that if a person, no matter his age, took the time to ask for his signature or the answer to a question, it was his obligation to react in kind.

There was on subject which Jim Thorpe never mentioned and which we never inquired about in the years that we were friends. That was his being deprived of his Olympic gold medals after his sensational, all-around dominance of the 1908 Games. It was as if we had an unwritten agreement that the subject would never be brought up. For that man Thorpe walked with a tremendous pride, and his greatest pride was his ancestry and his second greatest was the land in which he lived and to which he gave so much of his life. Therefore this public castigation in which they took away those material things which he cherished the most was, and no mistake about it, the greatest hurt he ever sustained. No, we never once discussed it because there was no reason to. You don't busy yourself in another man's privacy, and that was a closed door. But the memory of what was back of that door would live with Thorpe for as long as he lived.

Our infrequent, off-the-cuff chats in the lower Main Street bistro were strictly memory builders. You sat in awe of this great man, who was also a great guy, yet you marveled at the way he seemed to become one with you as you visited along. One of the things that endeared him to me was his devotion to children, for it has always been one of the primary joys of my life to call all children friends and have them call me the same.

One night, after we chewed the fat past the hour of midnight, Big Jim told us a story of a little boy which Healy and I have retold many, many times to groups throughout the area. It probably best describes Thorpe's attitude, his dedication, and his warmth, and there has never been a time in the history of the world that this story's lesson couldn't teach us all a lot.

Johnny, aged eight, was a fine, likeable, intelligent youngster who, in most things, was also cooperative. However, and not to his discredit because none of them start perfect, thank goodness, Johnny had one flaw in his armor. He never straightened up his room before he went off to school. His mom tried every conceivable type of discipline and punishment, but she could not get through to him the necessity of being neat with that room of his. Then, one day, an idea hit her full face. She spotted a large map of the world. Then she proceeded to cut it, á la jigsaw puzzle, into many, many pieces. These she placed in a box and then she sat and waited for her young son who, up until that morning, was still batting a thousand.

Along about half-past three, Johnny came marching home as usual. His mom met him at the door and continued his march right on up to his room. She closed the door and sat Johnny down. Then she said, "I have in this box a large map of the world cut into many pieces. You will put this map together and all of the time you are doing that you will be thinking of why you are doing it and why you are in here and not outdoors playing with your friends." She placed the pieces on a table, gave Johnny the straight eye, and said, as an exit line, "When you have finished with this and placed the map back in the box you may straighten up your room and come down to me in the living room." Then she closed the door with only an infinitesimal suggestion of skepticism but a loud crash of hope.

Ten minutes by the clock and Johnny was at his mother's side in the living room. He handed her the map and she appeared to be in a slight degree of shock. She said, "How is it possible for you to put this map together in less time than it took me to cut it up?" Johnny, with that little worldly-wise smile a kid will give you now and then, said, "Well, Mom, you see I noticed something when I started to put it together. On the other side of the map there is a big picture of a little boy. So all I did was put the little boy together and the world came out right."

Jim Thorpe pushed his huge frame erect and bade us a good night. Chuck looked at me and I looked back at Chuck. Then we both smiled. Then we went home. Our kids were waiting.

JOE McCARTHY

In the fall of 1943, shortly after the New York Yankees had won their seventh American League pennant in eight years under Joe McCarthy, CBS paid a special tribute to McCarthy on a coast-to-coast hookup testimonial. The program originated in New York, with Joe's participation coming from the WGR studios here in Buffalo. CBS asked me to handle the McCarthy interview, and I will always remember that day and that broadcast for one very special reason. Joe and I had become friends right after 1939, which, as you will recall, was the year I joined with WGR. McCarthy, then as now, was a resident of the western New York area although today he resides in a home just touching on the city limits of Buffalo instead of in his midtown Gates Circle dwelling where he and his beloved wife, Babe, lived during those years. His house was open at all hours to the guys who plied a sports trade whether they were involved in radio or newspaper work and whether he was at home or not, Babe was always there to sit and chat and open a bottle of beer.

During the course of that CBS interview, I asked McCarthy if he would list the names of some of the truly great men who had either played for him or against him. Joe, who wouldn't then and won't today name the greatest of any player or any game ("It's such a silly thing to even suggest"), did run off a list of top men including catchers, infielders, outfielders, and pitchers. When he came to great right-handers, he called off three or four. And when he came to the lefties, he said, ". . . and there was that Lefty Grove and who could ever have been greater than Ralph Hubbell?" Then he looked at me, with the strangest look, and said, "Of course I meant Carl Hubbell." It was the first and very last time that the error was made that way. Hundreds of times I have been referred to as Carl, the incredible New York Giant, but it was, I am sure, the only time Carl was tagged as Ralph. If the mistake was made in my favor just once, at least it was done in the grand manner by one of the true greats of all baseball time, Joe McCarthy—and coast-to-coast at that.

From that mistake to this minute, Joe McCarthy and I have been the closest of friends. Having spent an hour with him in his den of a thousand memories at his home on Ellicott Creek Road in Tonawanda, New York, just this morning, I can tell you that he is bright-eyed and alert—and, man, is he ever alert. At age eighty-seven, he remains vitally interested in the world at large and the game that he so dominated for so long and to which he gave so much of his life.

This man, who managed the Yankees from 1931 through 1945, is so vitally alive and human that just being with him is an inspiration in itself. Throughout the years, I have found that which most reporters find—that the truly great people are truly great in heart as well as in their abilities. The big ones are the ones who will always take time and who are never too busy for a person no matter how insignificant that man may be. A case in point with Joe McCarthy: One day when I was in New York and wanted to see Joe and ask him a couple of questions, I called him at the Commodore Hotel, and in answering the phone he showed his delight in receiving my call. When I asked him if I could see him for a few minutes, he didn't hesitate, he didn't beg off because he was in a special session with Ed Barrow, the president of the Yankees. His voice never skipped a beat as he said, "Come on along and just walk in." When I arrived and knocked on his door, he opened it and sure enough there was Mr. Barrow and there, too, in conference with MCarthy were Billy Evans, one of the great umpires of all baseball time, and Bob Cobb, the owner of the famed Brown Derby Restaurant in Hollywood and president of the Hollywood Stars of the Pacific Coast League. Joe introduced me to each man, identified me, and asked me to sit in. When the meeting ended, he took me to lunch.

Years later, when he was invited by the city of Olean to be guest of honor at a huge baseball ceremony, he called me on the phone and asked me to drive down with him. We—or he—were met at the city limits and there, awaiting Joe, was a gaily decorated convertible. But when he was ushered to the car and it became obvious that he was to ride in style on top of the back seat, he called a quick halt. He said, "Hubbell gets over here and rides with me or this car doesn't move." And for the entire day and through the night and thence back home he wouldn't budge without me. You were his friend not for what you could do for him but for what he could do for you, and his philosophy has never changed.

Joe McCarthy never played major-league baseball. He managed the Louisville team of the American Association from 1919 through 1925, and the following year went to the Chicago Cubs. He was replaced as manager by Rogers Hornsby in September 1930 and went on to the Yankees the next year. In his twenty-eight years as a manager, ending his career with the Boston Red Sox, only one McCarthy team ever finished out of the first division and that was when Louisville finished sixth in 1922. What made this man great? Why, if a man was a genius as a manager, wasn't he good enough to play the game he knew better or at least as well as any man who ever lived?

Marse Joe says, "Simply because I wasn't good enough. It is that simple. But that didn't mean that I couldn't recognize the talents of men who were good enough and then develop those talents." Three great instances of McCarthy's uncanny perceptiveness were Tony Lazzeri, Joe Gordon, and Red Rolfe. All three went to the Yankees as qualified, potentially brilliant, shortstops. Yet not one of the three came to world fame at that position. Lazzeri and Gordon, as the world knows, were second basemen, while Red Rolfe came to his greatness as one of the most brilliant of third sackers. "When I told Rolfe he could be a great third baseman, other baseball men thought I was daffy," Joe will tell you. "But Red couldn't go to his right and throw the long throw. At third, he went to his left, and he could throw from there with the best of them. As for Gordon, Joe came along when Lazzeri was just beginning to fade, and even youngsters know how great those two were." Joe smiled and said, "I remember Rolfe on the first ball that was hit to him the first day he played third. It skipped as he went to grab it, and it hit him squarely in the eye. He had the fattest eye you ever saw in your life. He used the other one to give me a good, long look. But he sure was a helluva third baseman, wasn't he?"

There is a priceless aura that seems to envelope the man MCarthy. When the last hurrah had heralded the departure of this man who occupies one of the most honored rooms in Cooperstown, he and Babe settled quietly into a peaceful existence at the farm on Ellicott Creek Road not far from Buffalo. Your footsteps should lead you there one day. The way is simple and the sign says, "Welcome."

You won't find Babe McCarthy there anymore, for she died

131

five years ago—a year that marked the fiftieth year of marriage for the celebrate couple.

You will find Joe, however, and you will feel, after just a few minutes of visiting, that this is a place set apart from all and this is a place, in a world that seems to know no peace, that welcomes and warms you and suggests that you bide awhile and suggests you come back again. Joe McCarthy doesn't live alone. Fred and Marie Richard live in what once was a caretakers' house that Joe has had done over completely. They share their lives and find happiness in the sharing. It was at this very place that our Peter and Phil came as starry-eyed visitors in the long ago and where Joe taught them how to throw a ball correctly. Years later, when I took Emmy out for a visit, Joe said, "Let me see you throw." When she threw, like a girl, Joe said, "Hey, you have to throw it this way." Together they worked on throwing a ball with both of them, each a kid in his own right, loving every second of it. Joe and Babe were never blessed with children, which explains to a great extent Joe McCarthy's fanatical interest in all kids. He said that each week's mail still brings requests for autographs. "They get my address from Cooperstown," said the squire, "and send along those cards. So I sign 'em and send 'em back."

Joe McCarthy wasn't good enough to play major-league baseball. No, all he did was to take the men who had the basic ability and make them great!

BABE RUTH

It was in 1927 that I first met Babe Ruth. Oh, no, not person to person or anything like that. I met him as all youngsters did—in the bleachers at Yankee Stadium, in the house that the Babe built. That year which was his record-setting year of sixty sky-high home runs was my Junior year in high school in Brooklyn and these many years later it won't make one iota of difference to a single soul if I reveal the fact that I, and my cronies, spent our spring and early fall hours riding the subway from Brooklyn to the Bronx. We didn't fool anyone then either. School could wait and it was a lucky thing because school did wait. All events waited for Babe Ruth.

Unless you actually lived in proximity to the great one—you can't really appreciate what this legend of a man meant to the workaday world or the world of sports. The man, who came out of a Baltimore orphanage to become a greatness who surpassed the sports stature of any man before or since, was a pitcher for the Boston Red Sox when the celebrated scandal of the Chicago American League club rocked, and almost ruined, the game in the years 1919-1920. History has chronicled the infamy of that horrendous crime against orgainzed baseball. The same history also tells of the wonder of the sport's resurrection and of the unalterable fact that two men rose from decent obscurity to nurse the sick and accused baby back to health and to ultimately establish it as the most stable of all sports dominions in the nation.

One was the dour-visaged, slump-shouldered, crushed-hat wisp of a man named Kenesaw Mountain Landis. The other was Babe Ruth. Landis was a judge who became famed for his fearless handling of all cases without fear of recrimination from any of the wounded parties no matter how powerful they were. Ruth was a left-handed pitcher with the Red Sox and about the best pitcher in the game during that time. But it was obvious Landis wasn't going to lead baseball back into the sun-light sitting on a federal court bench. And it was just as obvious that Ruth wasn't going to make the best use of his fantastic charisma as a one-appearance-every-four-days pitcher on the mound. Baseball paid Landis a more than substantial sum to create the position of "Commissioner of Baseball" while Ruth, who had demonstrated a fine ability to hit pitches out of parks, was sacked as a pitcher and installed as a right-fielder. History has told all who can read that these transitions almost ordained, were the one-two punch that baseball needed for survival.

Kenesaw Mountain Landis, in truth, came off the bench to administer baseball from his front-office throne. He did not ease into his new job. He was a fist-pounding tyrant from his very first day on the scene, and his every move was characteristic of a self-dedication that was almost too incredible to believe. Landis made every dictator in a long line of dictators look like a mealy-mouthed bum. As for the clubowners, who today run the commissioner, they quailed at the sight of the man they had installed to reestablish the credibility of a game that was almost dragged into filthy submission. But you had better believe they sat at his feet.

George Herman Ruth's story, told so many times that you could probably write it for me, was part of my growing up. He was a baseball genius and could be called the closest thing to the greatest performer of all time. He was a great pitcher, as the record book indicates, he was a great hitter, ditto, but he may have been the greatest as a defensive right-fielder. It was said of the Babe, once people could separate his hitting proclivities from his defensive ability, that he never threw a ball to the wrong base, which simply meant that, with all of his attributes, he had the instinct of greatness which sets the great apart from the very good.

It was always my thinking that Babe Ruth's supreme contribution to baseball, beside his leadership, was in his refusal to grow up. The kids loved him, adored him, idolized, and sought to emulate him because he simply never grew up. He always had time for them, never refusing anyone a single request, and he owned them all. But even in his adult living, in his activities away from the actual game itself, the Babe was a child at heart. That is why, and this I have always believed, Ruth never was given the big chance at managing that he so dearly yearned for and believed by rights, was his. But Ruth, a master of his own individual art, never would have cut the mustard because he would never have been interested in running an entire team. He had trouble enough managing his own affairs. Life was a great big game to Babe Ruth and the adulation that the world showed him was his main diet. Managers—the great ones—are born strategists. As Ruth was created to play the game with the ability and the instinct of genius, so too was Joe McCarthy created in the same manner with the same ingredients to be a manager of genius. Yet Joe never played even one major-league game. That's a two-sided coin.

The chances are that you never saw Ruth play. But those of us who did see him never forgot him. He had a barrel-type body constructed on a pair of inch-round ankles with feet to match. He really looked less like an athlete and more like a bulbous and successful businessman than any guy I ever saw. His eyes, his timing, his strength—they were his stock in trade. His home runs gave the impression of a small balloon released into the air that wafted out of there by a breeze. So high did the ball rise and so long was it airborne that it seemed the Babe had come 'round to the plate before the ball found it's ultimate resting place. One day, one of them found safe haven in my vicinity, and several days later Ruth autographed it for me. I kept it for years, and then a couple of years ago I was asked to appear as an auctioneer on the educational channel in our town, and I toted the ball with me. That ball, signed simply "Babe Ruth," brought some $550 from the highest bidder, and that was forty-two years after the home run.

It was during my tenure at WGR in mid-forties that Ruth had a birthday and I wrote a special birthday tribute to him. Afterward we had a recording made, and it was sent to Ruth at his home in New York. Some two weeks later, there came a short letter of thanks and this, too, was signed simply "Babe Ruth." But what interested me most and what intrigues me most about the letter today is the stationary upon which it is written. At the top, in bold Yankee blue letters, there is BABE RUTH. Directly underneath and in the same blue but in far smaller letters is "New York." And that is all. That was the address of the man who belonged to the whole wide world and whose name kindled a spark in the heart of every youngster in the nation.

When Gabby Hartnett was managing the Buffalo club, a long while back, I asked him a question to this effect: "That day when Babe Ruth hit the home run in the series against your Chicago Cubs, did he, in truth, point to the exact spot before he hit the thing out of the park?" Hartnett smiled and said, "Why not let the legend live?" When I told him that I doubted very much if I, an obscure announcer, could destroy the legend, he laughed right out loud. "No, I guess you couldn't," he said. And Gabby told me his version of possibly the most famous "shot call" of all athletic time. "Ruth had a count of two balls and two strikes on him with Charley Root on the mound," said the great Cub catcher who was working back of the plate that day. "Our dugout was giving the Babe a real ride, but as always he was taking it in the great and jovial mood which never seemed to desert him. Just before he stepped in for another pitch, he looked over at our bench and as he did so he held up one finger which was pointed toward center field. Then he yelled, "I've still got a strike to go!" Hartnett then disclosed that it was on the next pitch that Ruth hit the homer which sailed out right at the spot where he had pointed. Thus was the legend created that Ruth actually pointed to where he would hit the homer.

If memory serves, Roy VanGraflan, who later worked in the International League, was the plate umpire that day and I asked Van about it and he disagreed with Hartnett's version claiming that Ruth actually did call the next shot. It was quite a controversy at the time and the fact that we all still discuss it pro and con must be that lingering doubt is still prevalent concerning the true version. But I go along with Gabby, "Why not let the legend live?" Besides, I think Babe called the shot. Certainly he was capable of it.

ARNOLD PALMER

In 1972, with the plush and not easily coerced Cherry Hill Club course in Fort Erie providing the backdrop, the annual Canadian Open Golf Championships were contested with methodical, somber, cumbersome Gay Brewer taking the individual honors. Lee Trevino was the defending champ, he had won the event as the first of his miracle hat-trick conquests in 1971, and Arnold Palmer and Gary Player were in the field with only Jack Nicklaus among the missing. Brewer buried each of his more famous foes in his easy-going fashion and walked off with the trophy and the big cut of the loot.

Palmer was the focal point of all eyes, the big draw and the rest of it, but he was off his game that week and you don't win at Cherry Hill if any part of your game deserts you. But Palmer, and it's the little things you notice, was the class man he has always been and in just one simple little incident he proved that again.

The night before the event started, Palmer and some others were chatting at an informal gathering of contestants, officials, reporters, and other hangers-on when he turned to a friend and asked, "Where is a good place to have dinner in these parts?" The friend also happened to be a friend of Al DiGiulio, who happens to be responsible for one of the finest restaurants in the world, the Club 31, in Buffalo. DiGiulio was present at the gathering and so the two were introduced. After the first round of the tournament, Palmer, who had promised DiGiulio that he would arrive sharply at 6:30 for dinner, checked in at the Club 31 at exactly half-past six, accompanied by his agent. He was delighted with the repast, as you would be, and lingered a little longer than does the usual guest, as you would also. He simply was having a good time. The next day, Palmer was waiting to hit a second shot and as he gazed at the crowd, he spotted his host from the night before. He waved, smiled, and yelled, "Hey, Al, that was a wonderful meal last night."

The second night found Palmer right back at the same place with the same, extremely satisfactory results. The tourney went on to its conclusion, the players departed, and the world—and how often it does this—continued to move along. About three days later, the postman brought Al DiGiulio a letter with the postmark, Latrobe, Pa. It was a hand-written note which told Al again of how fine was his food and the sender expressed, again, his gratitude for the courtesy he and his agent had been extended. And it was signed, simply, "Arnold."

Such a little thing along the way. Yet what a wonderfully warm story to tell about a man who, as one of the most famous athletes who ever lived, had the inherent good breeding to take time to send back his thanks. And here again, friends, we find that one of the reasons the great are great is because they take the time.

137

JIMMY DUNNIGAN

We Americans are downright suckers for success stories in sports or, I guess, success stories in any line of endeavor. In some respects, we could be called sadists because what we like most of all is to see a guy start from nothing, go all the way to the top, hit a lean period, and then, pulling out all of the stops, come back to his sun again. If this is a formula that is slightly bewhiskered, it is one of truth and also the saga of James J. Dunnigan, Keeper of the Keys of Dunnigan's Diggins.

Jimmy Dunnigan is the man who established Buffalo Raceway as one of the prime harness tracks in North America and then, in an effort to conquer new worlds, not only failed in Arizona, but lost all he had won in Hamburg, New York, as well. Dunnigan's dad was John J. Dunnigan, New York State senator, who also fathered pari-mutuel wagering in the Empire State. Jimmy matriculated at Notre Dame, which should give you some idea of the stature of the man, where he studied law and earned a degree and somewhere along the way managed a brief career as a collegiate speed skater. But when the college days were finished, the young man lost the desire for jurisprudence at about the time that he lost his heart to the challenge of establishing himself in the world of the trot and the land of the pace. Besides, there's no money to be made in speed skating. Jimmy settled on western New York for planting his seeds because, knowing the soil was rich and good, he knew that the trees would grow tall.

When I first met Dunnigan in 1941, I recall my reaction was not to extend a hand in greeting but to offer him the courtesy of a three-fingered salute. He looked so young and, being of small stature, appeared to be ready for a Boy Scout meeting. First impressions are important, and you needed no second introduction to Jimmy Dunnigan, young as he looked, to know that he came to play. And he brought with him a young lady, Lillian Cheeseman, so extremely efficient in all realms of administration that without her I sincerely doubt, and Dunnigan feels certain about this, that

Buffalo Raceway would have become successful. By the very nature of its conduct, it drew praise from the entire world of the standardbred.

The raceway swung wide its gates for the first time in 1942. It was just about five months after Pearl Harbor, and much doubt was expressed as to whether the venture could survive. For travel in every sport was restricted and especially so in spectator sports where fans depended upon their cars, and thus their gasoline, to get them to the arenas on time. Buffalo Raceway fought its way through 1942, and I'll always recall the first night when the mutuel handle for eight races totalled $25,000. The sport had the nature of a county fair, with the fans coming in thousands, toting their lunch boxes and wagering nickels. That night Jimmy staged a party for all members of the press and his staff, and the echo of that party is as faint as the sound of distant drums today.

Buffalo Raceway made it through its baptisimal year and then gas rationing put the sport right on the local sidelines in 1943. Dunnigan closed his shop, promised that he would be back, and Jimmy joined with Saratoga, Yonkers, and Roosevelt raceways to conduct the sport in the more fertile soil of New York City just to keep it breathing until the gas-rationing period ended. That happened in 1944 and—true to his pledge—the ex-speed skater from Notre Dame returned to Buffalo and never looked back.

Quite to the contrary, Dunnigan's Diggins, as I dubbed the raceway one evening—and the name stuck—grew in stature every year. Batavia Downs, with Pat Provenzano and Jimmy Marra at the dual controls, kept pace, and before the 1940s succumbed to the 1950s these two ovals, their discouragements and their setbacks almost a forgotten period of their expansion years, carried their banners with equal dignity and their successes became accepted facts both here and in the nation as well!

Jimmy Dunnigan was at his very peak, and he was, indeed, an exceedingly rich young man. But sometimes there is a false bottom to the plateau of success. Sometimes, once the victory has been achieved, a man will ask himself: ''Are there no more worlds to conquer? Is this all there really is? Do I just stand pat on this, count my money, and play golf and gin rummy and, when the spirit moves me, have a belt now and then?'' In short, Jimmy Dunnigan didn't seek success as a preamble to a life of idleness. He was too active, too imaginative, and too nervous just to sit by the side of the road.

During his battling years at Buffalo Raceway, Dunnigan purchased a plush home for his wife, Mary, and the four Dunnigan lads in Scottsdale, Arizona. Each winter, Jimmy would go back to Arizona and play golf and gin rummy and have a belt now and then. But he wearied of this nothingness, and he belted a bit too much. What came next was two-fold. He would build the world's most wondrous harness track in Phoenix as a wintertime brother for Buffalo Raceway, and he would quit drinking. He accomplished both, but he failed in one. Dunnigan built a racing plant in Phoenix second to none at the cost of many millions of dollars, and he never took another drink again as he promised himself that he would not.

Jimmy Dunnigan lost everything he had fought for when, in 1967, the track opened and closed the same year in Phoenix and he lost Buffalo Raceway, too. He tried to save them both, but he had tied them together and when Phoenix died Jim lost his grip on, and his title to, the raceway in Hamburg. He had shot for the moon, but was blinded by the eclipse. For Dunnigan—in his avid desire to succeed—simply lost sight of the fact that a race track is opened, and thus closed, by the two-dollar bettor. And that fellow only lives where industry, abundant industry, thrives. His raceway was twenty-six miles from the downtown area, and Phoenix is a place, or was then, to clear your sinuses and to retire. Retirees have either enough money, so gambling doesn't tempt them, or not enough money, so they can't afford it. So one day Jimmy Dunnigan woke up broke and then became what America considers the perfect success story: The man who is up, then down, and then comes in the stretch to win it all because he believes in himself so consummately that he never gives a thought to ultimate defeat.

For four years, Dunnigan, a sort of a modern-day Henry Armstrong, kept battling forward, never yielding, never taking no for an answer. Then, in the spring of 1972, a syndicate which he spearheaded was granted a harness-racing franchise at the Los Alamitos track in California. The Southern California Racing Association was born just thirty years after Dunnigan swung wide the gates at Buffalo Raceway. Los Alamitos was a smash success under an avalanche of super-wagering performances. The year 1973 saw the track in operation more than thirty weeks of the year, but this time, having made it for the second time, Jimmy Dunnigan won't settle for golf and gin rummy, accepting idleness as his only reward. This time he is running the affair as head man, and he answers to other men so that he keeps in harness and he keeps an agile, ever aggressive brain agile and aggressive.

The Keeper of the Keys at Dunnigan's Diggins is solvent again—solvent of mind and money. And those of us who know him best, who were the ones who tried to make him see the light when we simply knew that Phoenix was not his answer, who were told to mind our own business, who revel, today, in his conquest of the tortuous trail back, we are the ones who applaud because we are the ones who love him best and fought with him the hardest. Yet even we are the first ones to admit that only a man of rugged purpose, of self-dedication and equal self-denial could have possibly achieved what this man has achieved. Therefore we join the applause as the old key fits into the new lock and the door to a new future opens for James J. Dunnigan, fighting son of a fighting dad.

OLLIE CARNEGIE

Pearl Harbor changed the face of the world as World War II burst upon us. So deeply did the Japanese attack on Pearl Harbor cut into the lives of so many countries that it was believed that the United States would suspend baseball for the duration of the war due to the draining of baseball manpower and the problem of transportation as a result of the all-out war effort. President Roosevelt, however, in his famed "Green Light" speech, instructed Judge Kenesaw Mountain Landis, the high commissioner of the major leagues, to order his owners to continue to play the game as a morale boost to young Americans wherever they happened to be. And although it meant recruiting athletes who were too young to go to war, too old to go to battle, or too unfit for any type of service, the majors and the minors never missed a game. Judge Landis said, "There is no question but that for the duration this will be the worst baseball we have ever played under the guise of major professionalism. But you will be pleased to remember that it will still be the best baseball in the world, the whole wide world." It became obvious that it was the worst when, in one of the war years, the St. Louis Browns, long-since deceased, won their only pennant in history.

Since it was necessary to restrict travel, Landis decreed that spring training would continue, but he established new boundaries. No team could train west of the Mississippi or south of the Mason-Dixon line, and it didn't take a geography map to ascertain that we had said farewell, at least for awhile, to Florida, as others kissed California a similar, and temporary, goodbye. In the two years that we stayed out of the sun, Buffalo trained one year in Hershey, Pennsylvania, and the second year in Hagerstown, Maryland. And of those two training years there is one memory that not only rates as the most poignant of that time but it is one of the most memorable incidents of the many years which saw me at the speaking end of a baseball play-by-play mike.

Landis had issued a call to all former ball players, not otherwise engaged, to lend a hand in the all-out effort to maintain baseball's pace during the war years. And they flocked back and they played their rusty brand of ball but they made it stick because they were champions when they retired and, if rust had set in those bones, when they returned the fire of desire and the willingness to cooperate had not diminished to any noticeable degree. And one such player was Ollie Carnegie.

Ollie played for Buffalo from 1931 to 1941. During his career he was the siege gun for all Bison teams, and he carried the deadliest, most potent bat in the International League. Ollie was thirty when he started his career so that when he quit he was starting his forties and when, in 1943, he decided it was his turn to pull an oar, he was halfway through fifty. But he hadn't gained an ounce of fat, his wrists were as big as ever, and his eyes were as clear.

Stiggy, Harris, and Hartnett, weary of the cold in Hershey that March, moved the club to Baltimore to continue training since it was two degrees warmer in Crab Town and also it was the spot where we were to open the season. We played our exhibitions against the Curtis Bay Coast Guard club and against the Senators, who trained at Fort Meade, which brings us to the day, the place, the game, and the incident.

Fort Meade is just one open acreage of parade ground, or so it appeared to us then. No fences, no grandstand. The eight thousand soldiers who watched our game that day sat all around the field, and though they would ship out the next day for unknown combat areas the kids gave no thought to any tomorrow. They were American boys watching America on parade—playing baseball. Washington was an established club, and they had seen the Senators several times. Buffalo, being a minor-league team, had many lesser lights needing public-address identification. Each Bison player was introduced during hitting practice, and when the announcer, a bright, young major, came to Carnegie's name he gave it the old build-up. "Greatest Bison hitter of all time, International League home-run king, holder of the runs batted in records for team and league, etc., etc.," ". . . and, men, Ollie Carnegie is forty-five years old."

That was it. That was all eight thousand G.I.'s had to hear—a guy playing pro ball who was older than most of their fathers. And let me tell you, friends, just let me set you straight, once Ollie's age had been announced, those kids gave him one of the most merciless (albeit in good fun) word maulings that any athlete ever had to endure. But you never guessed it by looking at Carnegie that day. His face was grim, and his features resembled a relief map.

143

The game started, and Washington was using a young phenomenon by the name of Marino Pieretti who was a steamy-fast right-hander with a desire to make the club.

When Carnegie came up for the first time, Pieretti literally blew him down on three strikes, and as he went back to the bench Ollie was given his first real taste of G.I. razz. The next time he came up, the Buffalo immortal hit a long fly which the third baseman gathered in. The third time Ollie hit back to the pitcher and was thrown out by fifteen feet. By now the din was so thunderous that you expected rain at any moment—and out of a crystal clear sky at that.

Then Ollie came out for round four. Washington, also teetering with as much age as youth, had a left fielder named Jake Powell who had also earned his spurs and his fame, retired and returned to help. When Carnegie hit his home runs in Buffalo he hit them on a line to the left and the fielder many times thought the ball was marked with his own name and he'd just stand there waiting for the end of the flight. But about thirty or forty feet before the ball came to the waiting fielder, it would suddenly take off as if it had hit a ski slide. There was never actually any way of knowing how far a Carnegie blast actually went because beyond Offerman Stadium there was a house with a tin roof and the small object would smack against it and carom away.

In the eighth, Pieretti had Buffalo by some six runs, and the game was awasting. Whether he had compassion beyond his years or whether he just made a bad pitch will never be known. But with a two and two count, the pitcher threw Ollie a waist-high curve that, when he is 145, he will hit out of a dark room. The ball screamed about three feet above the third baseman's head and took off for Jake Powell. But with Powell, that day, everything wasn't Jake. The ball hit the air slope and zoomed up and over his head. Powell just couldn't run back to the fence, watch it sail up and on, say something about the pitcher, and then return to his position. Not in Fort Meade, he couldn't. Not when a Carnegie-tagged home run flew healthy over his head he couldn't. Jake had to go get the ball. Meanwhile the suddenly emerged hero of this piece, Mr. Carnegie, had reached second and was ready to stop. But he couldn't stop because there was Powell still chasing the ball. He went into a three-quarter limp and a half dog-trot and made it to third, ready to die. But Ollie couldn't even die because the puffin' Powell was stll tracking down a baseball which, by now, Jake had referred to in many different terms.

So Ollie Carnegie WALKED into the plate. As he started toward the dugout he stood, suddenly, stock still. For eight thousand G.I.'s were standing holding their helmets to the sky, and they gave that man that day the greatest acclaim that any athlete could ever possibly have been given. Cy Kritzer, my reporting buddy, and I looked at Carnegie. His shoulders were straight, his legs bowed, his cheeks streaked with tears. It was as if it were the benediction of a truly great baseball career.

Ollie Carnegie is seventy-two today, and he lives quietly here in Buffalo. We had lunch the other day, and you can bet we reminisced. When we mentioned Washington in the spring of 1943, Carnegie smiled and said nothing. Then I said, "Ollie, do you know how far you hit that ball?" Ollie said, "It went, with carry and roll, 680 feet." Funny about that, but I knew it too, 'cause when the kids were gone we measured it. No, we can't bring those year back, but isn't it nice to know that no one can ever take them from us?

13

We Are No Longer Strangers

THE TITLE FOR THIS BRIEF AND FINAL chapter is possibly the most significant single thought expressed during our walk together. For we started as strangers and we finish as friends. Thus, if our visit means nothing else at all, it most certainly means the accomplishment of friendship and it takes no towering genius to realize that friendship, once a common denominator in the world, is a condiment that the world is more than a trifle short on at the present time.

Being quite obviously a sentimentalist—Tem always said that there is nothing wrong at all with a good clean, tear—I feel parting more than most people. It is unmistakably true that a person dies a little each time he says goodbye. Yet what is memory for? To be able to recapture, any time we feel that we want to, the feeling of friendship even though the friend has walked another path or, as he must, the final path.

As we come to this separating fork in our road there are many thanks I'd like to give. To men such as Jack Kemp who wrote the introduction; to Chuck Healy who closes our book; to Lou Schaefer who was first to be my friend at Westminster; to Ann for saying "yes" in the long ago; to Charley Murray for suggesting we say nice things of meaningful people and forget the rest; to

Stiggy for accepting the role of vicarious father to all of us who needed his wisdom; to Max Robinson for his lasting lessons in courage; to Peter, Phil and Emmy for agreeing to grow with us after our initial acceptance of them; to the thousands of athletes who played; to the hundreds of athletes who were my friends; to the legion of listeners and readers who heard me and read me through the 40 year trail which seems, at journey's end, shorter than a 40 yard dash; to Tem—who made it all possible in the first place. In large measure do my thanks go to those two slick chicks, Dame Fortune and Lady Luck, who teamed with Almighty God to bring joy and happiness and meaning to the House on Huntington. May we all part in affection and may we know peace—and in our time. . . .

And now, and by your leave, I go. For I hear a distant sound as that of music playing. Now, of a sudden, the music repeats and repeats and repeats as if the needle, in some memorial way, has caught a record groove.

My reason for rushing back is clear for I have a rendevous with the ghost of Frank Meyers and, together, we have a date at which time we will fashion a young man's every tomorrow, tomorrow, tomorrow, tomorrow, tomorrow, tomorrow..........

Afterword

F. SCOTT FITZGERALD ONCE WROTE THAT you don't write because you want to say something, you write because you have something to say.

Ralph Hubbell's sixty-plus years, forty of them devoted to people of the world of sports, have given him much to say, as you have discovered in the preceding pages.

It was my pleasure to share some of his experiences as he walked and talked always with an attentive and retentive mind, to the sports greats and near-greats. However, you didn't have to be a star to attract his interest, and some of his better tales are those he tells about many who never made any headlines whatsoever. That is the unique quality of your author who is fully at home with the Ben Hogans and Marse Joe McCarthys as well as the Ma Millers and Walter Drozs.

This man's life has not been devoid of problems. Yet he learned early to treat all disasters as incidents and none of the incidents as disasters. This has enabled him to become the compassionate, warm human being he is.

During my college fraternity days at Syracuse, we enjoyed a tradition which we called "after glow." Following a major event or fraternity dance, the brothers would gather in the main hall of the frat house to share the highlights and the personal happenings of the evening over a cold beer or a mellow wine. My personal friendship with Ralph Hubbell is now in it's twenty-sixth year. Reading *Come Walk With Me* and recalling many of the moments he and I shared has brought back that same warmth of the college after-glow days. It's a warmth that is comfortable and reassuring.

Has Ralph now told it all? Not in any way can this be true. His life, if not quite as exciting, is fuller, busier, richer than ever. He continues to explore new avenues as he forever seeks to add to his treasury of amusing and heart-warming stories, and his insatiable devotion to all people will never let him rest until he is certain that he has met them all.

Hubbell has discovered that one who keeps on learning not only remains young but constantly becomes a more valuable human being regardless of any inroads that age may bring. We hope that Ralph will let us walk with him again. No trip could be more delightful—not even these years he has allowed us to share with him.

–Chuck Healy